Sunday Adelaja
Only God can save Nigeria: what a myth?
©2016 Sunday Adelaja
ISBN 978-1-908040-41-1

Copyright © Golden Pen Limited
Milton Keynes, United Kingdom. All rights reserved
www.goldenpenpublishing.com

Cover design by Alexander Bondaruk
Interior design by Igor Kotelnikov

© Sunday Adelaja, 2016,
Only God can save Nigeria: what a myth?
Milton Keynes, UK:
Golden Pen Limited, 2016

WHAT OTHERS ARE SAYING ABOUT THIS BOOK

"Only God Can Save Nigeria, What A Myth"... is a masterpiece, a revolutionary thought-provoking, compelling and challenging book. The notion that God is going to come down and change Nigeria's precarious situation is absurd and contrary to any logical reasoning.

In my entire years of ministry as missionary dedicated to building people's lives and effecting changes to nations, I have never read a book written with such a passion, intensity and authority. This is not another religious manual, this book is beyond all established religious procedures. This book will challenge every fiber of your being, transform your mindset and elevate you to the class of people that pioneer change in the affairs of our beloved country.

Dr Sunday Adelaja is not only a revolutionary genius but also a trailblazer, an innovator, a pathfinder, and a generational figure. His book offers a determined analysis of the cause, the nature and the root of Nigeria's problem. It also provides insightful solution and practical steps to restoring the glory of our great country, Nigeria. A must read for every Nigerian awaiting the redemption and salvation of our beloved country.

REV JOSEPH OYEWOLE,

FOUNDER OF THE TRIUMPHAL ENTRY MISSIONS INTERNATIONAL (T.E.M.I.), PRETORIA, SOUTH AFRICA.

Pastor Sunday Adelaja touches the heartbeat of God with this his latest book. As we cry for the transformation of Nigeria, it is clear that it is in our hands, the hands of the

Church, the body of Christ, because God has put it there. Pastor Sunday exposes the myth that 'Only God Can Save Nigeria', and rebukes us from throwing our hands up in frustration waiting on God to rescue us. He illustrates from the story of Dubai, how men using their God given talents can make a remarkable difference.

I hope as you read this book, it will open your eyes to your role and encourage you to step out and fulfil it. I know that Pastor Sunday's singular objective in writing this is to see Nigeria transformed.

PASTOR WALE ADEFARASIN

GENERAL OVERSEER, GUIDING LIGHT ASSEMBLY
WORLDWIDE

Dr. Adelaja's new book, "ONLY GOD CAN SAVE NIGERIA: WHAT A MYTH!" echoes the cry of the Nigerian anthem- "Arise, O' compatriots Nigeria's call obey." Propelled by love for his fatherland, Adelaja challenges his primary constituency, the body of Christ to take up the transformation of the Nigerian state as a necessary spiritual responsibility. All through the book, he stresses the fact that the destiny of a nation does not lie in God's Hand, but with her citizens.

Drawing references from the Scripture and his active participation in the building of modern Ukraine, Adelaja proves that the Gospel of the Kingdom is not about Christians seeking selfish miracles from God's Hand, but the Church leading the front line in national rebirth.

This book introduces a new meaning to the term missionary, as it challenges every citizen to identify and take up a particular sector of society as his personal mission field. This concept is both radical and breathtaking.

Indeed, God is not a Nigerian, but the creator of Nigeria. And never has the Almighty independently built any nation without the dedicated input of her citizens. For this to happen in Nigeria, Adelaja proffers practical steps he has tested through his experience in Ukraine. Dr Adelaja's antecedents eminently qualify him to write this book. Therefore, I recommend it as a blueprint for transforming not only Nigeria but also any nation in the world.

NWADIASHI IKE. A.

CEO, WAD & ASH LIMITED,

(ENTREPRENEURSHIP AND LEADERSHIP CONSULTANT)

'This book will hit some raw nerves on both ends of the spectrum – good and bad. It will spur some, and sour some up! Timely, necessary, catalyst'

CHRISTIE BATURE OGBEIFUN

180 DEGREES REHAB CENTRE, PORT HARCOURT.

Congratulations, you are holding the solution to Nigeria's problems. In this book, Pastor Sunday Adelaja provides a pathway for national transformation through kingdom minded Christians. The principles outlined in this book are simple practical steps to transforming any nation, and Nigeria is no exception. I see people being set free from the mental enslavement propagated by distorted religious doctrine.

In a simple and compelling way, Dr. Sunday Adelaja has busted the commonly used phrase "Only God Can Save Nigeria". Using both scriptural and historical examples, he makes his point clear, leaving the readers with no room for doubt. He has also outlined in practical ways not only how each one of us can identify our area of calling and gifting, but also how we can spring into action to bring about the much needed transformation in

Nigeria. Responsibility has been clearly assigned to the churches and individuals alike. Without any ambiguity, we all have a part to play to bring about the much needed positive change we desire to see in Nigeria.

This book is so timely at this stage in our national life. In it lies the solution to our national problems. It is my take that this book should be made available to every Nigerian. Even if this means distributing free copies of the book in our schools, churches, government and private offices and every congregation of people. Every Nigerian has to read this book. As you read along, your mind will be stretched through the God-given principles outlined in this book.

Dr. Sunday Adelaja is a man with one message, which has been consistent over the years - the transforming message of the gospel of the Kingdom of God. He epitomises kingdom values and has been used by God to transform nations through practical application of kingdom principles. This book is not just some theoretical ideology but it outlines tested principles that has been used and is being used to transform the nation of Ukraine.

I therefore implore you not just to read through like any other book, but resolve to apply these principles in your life and in your ministry and you will surely see God work tremendously through you in a personal and powerful way to bring about a change in your life and country. God bless!

DIEPERE TAIGER

CHAIRMAN BOARD OF TRUSTEE
KINGDOM AMBASSADORS GRACE CENTRE

Sunday Adelaja

ONLY
GOD
can save
NIGERIA:
What a Myth!

CONTENTS

Foreword

The heaven, even the heavens, are the
Lord's; But the earth He has given to
the children of men. (PSALM 115:16)

This scripture confirms God's action when He created Eden, the beautiful garden and told Adam to tend and keep it - Genesis 2: 15

It is obvious that the church in Nigeria has abandoned her responsibility and is telling God to add our responsibilities to His. God did well when he created this beautiful earth for us, as well as all that would be needed in maintaining it. We know that we are created in God's image and likeness as the Bible tells us. And since we have His likeness, we are supposed to do what he does - creating and inventing things useful for man.

It is from this unique nature that men have derived the knowledge and skill to create ships moving on water, automobiles moving on road and airplanes travelling in the sky. This knowledge was created with man regardless of their colour, race or faith belief. I am very excited that the world is making great success in technology and general invention in things that are useful and make life convenient for man.

Looking at the situation facing Nigeria, I am really challenged and compelled to add my voice to Pastor Sunday Adelaja's in asking Nigerians to arise and take the bull that the Lord has given us by the horn and do the needful. Our endless complaints about the failure of Government to deliver must come to an end as we take responsibility for the 'garden' (Nigeria) that God has given us.

It is a reality that many nations that are not seriously disposed to religion or "our most cherished faith" are doing so well. Holiday destinations have shifted massively to the Middle and Far East countries. Reasons, the people are doing their bits. Their economies are doing well and infrastructures are multiplying daily, yet we who claim to be the children of the God that created the earth are wallowing in unprecedented setback. While we are singing "only God can save Nigeria", God is saying only the church can fix Nigeria!

In total agreement with Pastor Sunday, I am challenging the church including myself to discover our special area of influence and turn the ugly tide around. If the church does not arise, we would be in trouble with God. Joseph, a type of the church was the solution in Egypt. Esther and her uncle Mordecai were instrumental to the deliverance of an entire race. Can I ever forget the four Hebrew young men who distinguished themselves under Nebuchadnezzar? The Bible tells us that at the end of their training, the King personally interviewed the graduates and found them ten times better than the rest.

The church is the salt of the earth and light of the world as Jesus said. Joseph did not have to be a prophet, pastor or evangelist to solve Egypt's problems. The four Hebrews (Daniel, Shadrack, Meshack and Abednego) were neither ordained deacons or elders anywhere in Babylon, but they took God along with their skill and became the brains behind the only world power of their day.

According to apostle Peter, all the grace needed to affect nations has been packaged in the New Testament believer when he says, "But you are a chosen race, a royal priesthood, a dedicated nation, [God's] own *purchased, special people, that you may set forth the wonderful deeds and display the virtues and perfections of Him Who called you out of darkness into His marvelous light" - 1 Peter 2:9. God has created and packaged these virtues and skills in us not to use in heaven, but on earth where we are called to shine.

Our course of action now is to begin to use our vocation as

platform for the kingdom rather than limiting ourselves to our mere weekly religious activities that are constricted to the four walls of our denominations. Time is no longer on our side. We or I should say YOU, are the solution! YOU are the answer! We should stop asking God to do what He asked us to do!

Please read this special epistle to the church in Nigeria and tell others about it. It's not too late to turn things around.

ABRAHAM OLALEYE

THE BISHOP OF ABRAHAM'S
EVANGELISTIC MINISTRY, AEM

Introduction

*"Religion is the sigh of the oppressed crea-
ture, the heart of a heartless world, and
the soul of soulless conditions. It is the
opium of the masses"* (KARL MARX)

In remembering this quotation, my heart bleeds for the masses of the Nigerian descent who have unconsciously given true meaning to this statement. Or why else would we have a nation of able-bodied, highly industrious and largely intelligent people live as though they were the very cursed of God. Oh, why would we have a nation of highly achieving and greatly distinguished people in various fields of life spread across the different nations of the world yet, have their own country in such a catastrophic quagmire. Can somebody please answer the question on why we have a nation of one of the most optimistic and cheerily positive people on earth live as defeated beings, frustrated and wretched people?

I'll tell you. It is because "Religion indeed has become the opium of the Nigerian masses". Much in the same way that people visit taverns and pubs and beer parlors in order to stupefy themselves, knock themselves out and escape the reality of whatever situation it is they are faced with, the Nigerian masses have also resorted to taking advantage of God. They have resorted to shifting all their responsibilities to the nation on Him; chanting the chorus "Only God can save Nigeria" as a way of escaping from the reality on ground. Hence, abdicating their responsibilities and fueling the notion that Nigeria's problem is acutely complicated and thereby irresolvable.

Nothing could be farther from the truth as there is no single problem facing Nigeria today that is complicated, convoluted or irresolvable. There is no single problem that Nigeria is facing today that cannot be surmounted and brought low if only the citizens of this great and illustrious nation will take up the gauntlet, rise to arms and face up to the situation on ground.

There are many other nations on earth today that have been in worse states than Nigeria (we will be exploring some of them in this book) has found herself in. But noteworthy is the fact that these nations have gone ahead to become the envy of the world today. All of these nations have become the hub of development, safety of lives and properties, booming economy, widespread high quality education, low corruption, political and economic stability, freedom for all her citizens, high quality lifestyle, low mortality rate, access to qualitative healthcare, excellent infrastructures, low unemployment rate and even much more. Sadly, these very things are the things that Nigerians pray, fast, cry and ask God to make happen for them. The very same things that they have in their power to bring about.

Indisputably, there is the role of God in the affairs of men but yet there is the role of man in the affairs of this world as well. Come to think of it what if Thomas Edison, the commercial light bulb inventor or Alexander Bell, the telephone inventor or the Wright brothers who built and flew the first aircraft decided to adopt the siddon look and pray mentality of the average Nigerian Christian, what would have happened to our world today without all their great inventions and discoveries.

Great Nigerians, brothers and sisters, my message to you today is that the answer to the Nigerian predicament lies in every single one of us. The answer to the insurgency, corruption, poverty, hunger, power issues, deplorable infrastructures, high unemployment rate, insecurity and all the other myriads of problems facing the nation of Nigeria rests in each and every one of us. It is my firm belief that each Nigerian has been solely packaged and inbuilt by God with the solution to at least one of the problems facing the country. And the earlier you identify and discover your own solution, the better for the common good of all.

Hence in this book, I will show you how to identify the solution that you have been specifically built to tackle and subdue for Nigeria. I will show you how that through the collective body of Christ (the church) in Nigeria we can unequivocally turn the fortunes of Nigeria around. In this book I will show how the Nigerian Christians can collectively bring about the most needed change, transformation and development that the masses so desperately desire without receiving help from the government or any foreign nation. Through this book, you will come to understand how every Nigerian including yourself has a unique relevance to contribute to the nation to free her from all her woes and turn her to the most desirable nation on earth.

The system to transform Nigeria that has been outlined in this book is not some outlandish, far from reality and impracticable model. Rather, it is a model that has been tried and tested and found to be true. This same model is what has made the church I pioneered – The Embassy of God for all nations practically infiltrate all the stratum of the Ukrainian nation such that Christians from our churches are some of the most influential personalities in the nation of Ukraine today. For real Christians from our church have become the major force that have driven the transformation of Ukraine and are still driving her transformation today.

Many of these Christians have gone ahead to occupy positions in government and all social spheres of the nation which has contributed to a radical development of this nation. This same model has been tweaked and modified to transform the Nigerian clime. This book is the answer to the years of unanswered prayers for change and transformation that Nigerians have so desperately craved for.

Times may change, people may change even methods could differ but principles are unchanging. It is my firm belief that through reading this book and applying its principles Nigeria will become great again through the collective efforts of all her citizen.

SUNDAY ADELAJA

FOR THE LOVE OF GOD, CHURCH AND NATION

PART 1

Confronting the Status Quo

CHAPTER 1

The Nigerian Religious Mindset

The Nigerian Religious Mindset

Sometimes when someone begins to question our religious status quo, the response one would often get would be something like "this guy is either backslidden or is not a Christian at all". However, I intentionally titled this book "ONLY GOD CAN SAVE NIGERIA" - WHAT A MYTH! I want the title to catch the attention of the readers so they could question their reasoning. I want to challenge a widely spread notion that we have and spur us to begin to look at things from a whole new perspective. So since I have your attention now, let's begin.

IS IT REALLY ONLY GOD THAT CAN SAVE NIGERIA?

Of course you do know that when we say "only God can save Nigeria" then we are indirectly saying that the reason Nigeria is the way it is right now is because God hasn't done something that He is supposed to do. But how correct is that notion? Is it really true that the reason Nigeria is where it is today is because God hasn't made that move to save her yet? This might be the reason behind the high level of religious involvement in Nigeria then.

Just in case you are not very familiar with the religious terrain in Nigeria, let me paint the picture for you here. Statistically speaking, there are at least 80 million Christians in Nigeria today.

The Institute of Social Research of the University of Michigan in the United States once carried out a study about Christianity and church attendance around the world. It was discovered that Nigeria has the highest rate of church attendance in the world! I mean Nigeria beats every single nation you can imagine in terms of how faithfully and judiciously her citizens attend church meetings.

Of more interest is the fact that this is a record the country has faithfully held from as far back as 1990 when the survey was first carried out until the last recorded one in 2013. That is about 23 years of consistent and faithful religious devotion! Hmmm! How interesting!

Nigeria boasts of some of the largest church auditoriums and Christian gatherings around the world today. We have the likes of the Faith Tabernacle at Ota, Ogun state that seats about 50,000 people (besides overflows) and still runs multiple services every Sunday. Not forgetting the fact that the construction of another 100,000-seater auditorium is under way right now.

We have the annual Holy Ghost Festival of the Redeemed Christian Church of God (RCCG) that also attracts millions of worshippers into a single location. In fact, the RCCG is currently constructing an arena that would be three kilometres wide and three kilometres long! That building is estimated to accommodate nearly twelve million people in a single gathering.

This is not to mention the ultra-modern auditorium of the Catholic Church of Transfiguration in Lekki, Lagos that cost a whopping $14 million to build. Or the National Ecumenical Center in Abuja seating about eight to ten thousand people at a cost of N2.6 billion ($20 million) as at the year of construction.

Noteworthy also is the fact that Nigeria also has a national mosque situated right on the independence avenue, across the National Christian Center. The facility costs a humongous sum of money and it houses a religious school, a library and a conference hall as well.

The Salvation Ministries aka Home of Success led by Pastor David Ibiyeomie is also constructing her 90,000-seater capacity auditorium now however that is not all. Dunamis International Gospel Center led by Pastor (Dr.) Paul Enenche and his wife are presently constructing a 75,000-seater capacity auditorium. The Mountain Of Fire and Miracles Ministries (MFM) is equally erecting her 500,000-seater capacity auditorium at the moment.

These are just a few of the several examples we could cite. So, am I against the crowd? Of course not. I am only painting the picture of what is obtainable in our nation for you. I have only mentioned these specific examples to give you an idea of how much Nigerians are attracted to religious gatherings and prayers week after week.

Untold thousands and hundreds of thousands of Nigerians get up early enough to attend services as early as 6am on Sundays. Many of them stay in churches for countless hours if not all day on Sundays. Several millions of Muslims also troop to the mosques and worship places on Fridays and other days as well.

It is in Nigeria you will find that every single day of the week is a day of church activity. From Monday prayer meetings to Tuesday bible studies and then Wednesday Mid-week services to Thursday workers meetings and Friday all night vigils. Then on Saturday, they return for rehearsals in preparation for Sunday services and then still be bewildered with meetings at the end of Sunday services.

Where else in the world do people attend services on Monday mornings? Where do you find people having as much religious holidays as we do in Nigeria? Where else do people have prayer and fasting programs stretching over a 100-day period with faithful worshippers showing up every day after work? What about fortnight prayer meetings that hold from 7am to 4pm on Mondays and has workers, students, skilled labourers and other professionals in various fields of life in attendance?

Then we wonder why the Church and Mosques haven't been effective in affecting the nation? We then turn around and utter our consolatory lingo "Only God Can Save Nigeria?"

Don't get me wrong here. There is really nothing wrong with prayer. It is just important for us to note that prayer is not the only requirement for a positive change in any society. Prayer alone is not what it takes to transform a nation.

Come to think about it, how much of those prayers and church attendance have translated into national development? How much of that attendance has affected the state of things in our nation? While we have faithfully maintained the top spot as the highest churchgoers around the world for more than 23 years in a row, our economy and all that we stand for has consistently taken a nosedive. Things have moved from bad to worse and from worse to worst for our dear country over time. Now, to make matters worse, we resort to the idea or philosophy that "Only God Can Save Nigeria!"

Come on here, which God are we really talking about? Which God are we waiting on? Was it the same God that helped nations like Japan, Singapore, Saudi Arabia, the United States and so on to build their countries? Was it the same God that helped turn Dubai from a city best described as a desert into the eye catching, world attraction it has become today? Was it God that turned Dubai into the fastest growing desert city in the world?

Actually, it is more interesting to know that the majority of these developments the world celebrates in UAE were put in place between the years 1990 and 2003. That is just about half of the period over which we have been named the country with the highest church attendance!

Would it be fair to say that while we were busy attending church services, other nations were developing? Would it be correct to say that while we were whiling away time in religious hickory dickory, other nations were developing and advancing? I mean, if God was responsible for the development of nations, shouldn't He have favoured those of us who were the most faithful to church services? Shouldn't He have favoured those of us who are more consistent in our attendance of church meetings?

The mere fact that our extreme religiosity and attendance to religious activities hasn't resulted in an automatic development of our nation should tell us something. It should tell us that the development of nations is not by how much or how well we attend church services or Muslim khutbah. The development of nations does not result when people sit back, do nothing and expect God to fix things for them.

This is the same reason why the majority of our citizens live in abject poverty today. They sit, hope, pray and even fast that the God that blesses people will one day look upon their faithfulness to church attendance and change their financial fortune. Meanwhile, the not so godly people are making waves. The not so churchy people are advancing and developing greatly. Christians have become so associated with poverty that it has become a standard for measuring poverty around the world. Hence, the phrase "as poor as a church rat".

Sift through the world's record of the richest men on earth today. How many of them are religious men? How many of them got there by their religious involvements and affiliations? Did you ever read that Bill Gates who has held the record of the richest man in the world for 16 out of 21 years was made so by God? Was it God that made our very own Aliko Dangote the richest in all of Africa? Or did you ever read that Dangote was a prayer warrior somewhere?

All these men and nations I have mentioned have gone ahead to build enviable lives and societies for themselves because they decided to take the opposite route to the one we have taken as a nation. They decided to be pro-actively productive instead of waiting for God to do for them what He has already enabled them to do!

> *"God and Nature first made us what we are, and then out of our own created genius we make ourselves what we want to be. Follow always that great law. Let the sky and God be our limit and Eternity our measurement."* (MARCUS GARVEY)

Oh how I wish that the Nigerian populace understood this! How I wish that we knew that the same God we are busy waiting for to change our country isn't going to do so. How I wish we knew that the answer to our endless vigils and prayers has always been with us.

Marcus Garvey was absolutely right when he said God has already made us what we are. And out of the genius that has been deposited in us, we ought to now make ourselves what we want to be. In other words, contrary to what most of us think, God is waiting on us to do something about our country. God is looking up to us to effect the changes we desire in our nation. He is counting on the ingenuity of our person and the abilities locked up within us to do just that.

So for as long as we stay idle and wait for God to come and do something about our country, nothing will happen. While we are busy looking up to God, we should also understand that on the other hand, God is waiting for us to do something as well. This explains why haven buried our heads in prayers and all manner of religious activities all these while, nothing has happened. We even transition from one government to the other and yet no notable change is taking place in the entire nation. In the midst of all our religious efforts, our youths are taking to all manner of vices and terrorizing our society.

Countless millions of Nigerians troop the churches and places of religious gatherings both on Sundays and every other days of the week. We pray, sing, dance and hear the supposed word of God and yet, that word is doing close to nothing in affecting our nation. Sometimes I do wonder what type of word it is we hear in our churches.

In all our attendance to church and our devotion to the mosques, we haven't been able to give birth to enough jobs to affect the unemployment rate in our country. We haven't been able to keep away children of school age from the streets where poverty has kept them. Young and promising chaps end up hawking for survival while we attend our sanctimonious services.

Isn't it surprising that armed robbery, fraud and corruption, the deplorable state of our roads, the electricity problem and every single issue that bedevils the Nigerian state seems to be progressing in the midst of our praying and waiting on God? It is really difficult not to ponder on the kind of God it is we really go to worship.

Every year, thousands of Nigerian Christians travel to Jerusalem and Rome on pilgrimage. Of course, the majority do so with financial support from the Government. Likewise thousands of Muslims travel on pilgrimage to Mecca every year and the Government at both state and federal levels provide billions of Naira in support of these religious trips. Ours is such a country of religious folks with little to no development!

Is it that we are not being taught the right things or is it that we have taken up the character of those Paul was writing to Timothy about when he said "…Ever learning, and never able to come to the knowledge of the truth." (2 Tim 3:7)

The question we should be asking ourselves is "how have all these affected our socio-economic life as a country"? The countries we envy and often holiday in, was this how they were built? Did they also wait for God to come and save their land or is it that our own case is so special that we have to wait on God and for God?

THE NIGERIAN UNDERSTANDING OF GOD AND PRAYER

Today, the average Christian has been raised to see God as an instrument to be used to fulfil all his selfish desires. We have been trained to believe that God exists for us rather than we for Him. As far as we are concerned, what else is God there for if not to listen to our long tirades in the name of prayer and grant every stupid request of ours?

Think about it for a moment, why else will a prostitute set to leave her house or brothel for the streets go on her knees and ask God to send good and wealthy customers her way? Don't let that surprise you because it is happening in Nigeria today!

Or how can a group gathered to discuss how to inflate contracts begin with an opening prayer or sometimes two opening prayers? Or how do we explain that politicians who gather to discuss how to rig elections also begin with prayer? What about the armed robbery gang that is set to go for an operation gathering to pray for God's favour before they set out?

In fact, the Nigerian Punch Newspaper of September 14, 2014 reported how some suspected armed robbers that had been arrested by the police confessed to habitually praying to God before they would embark on any robbery operation. When one of the armed robbers was questioned, among other things he said: "That is why we usually prayed to God before embarking on any operation. The prayer was for God to protect us and to bring only sinners our way so that those who were innocent would be spared."

WHAT A COUNTRY! WHAT A PEOPLE!

We are so religious and yet so ignorant of God! We are even worse than the Israelites of old whom the bible said only knew the acts of God but not his ways. We neither know his ways nor his acts yet we are acclaimed to be the most attendant to services. Christianity for us has been reduced to just attending services and nothing more. Yet the country is speedily progressing in the wrong direction. The only charts we top around the world are the charts of corrupt countries and poor nations meanwhile, there is a torrent of power lying within us. Yet all we know to say is that "Only God Can Save Nigeria" After which we promptly fold our arms and expect a miracle!

THE STORY OF MRS. FOLUKE

I remember the very touching story of one Mrs Foluke I got to know about. She was a banker in one of the banks in Nigeria. Based on her outstanding performance at work, she was promoted and transferred from Oshogbo to Ibadan. Of course, that came with greater responsibility but she wasn't bothered. She knew she was up to the task.

A few weeks after she got to Ibadan with her family, someone introduced her to a certain church. After her first visit there, she liked it and decided to stay there with her family. By the way, her husband was working abroad so she was also saddled with the responsibility of training their three children.

After a few weeks of attendance, some of the leaders in the church approached her. They asked her to join a group or two in the church to enable her effectively serve the Lord. Initially, she was reluctant because she didn't think she would have the time to commit to any of such considering her banking job's demand on her time. The church authority persisted in their request until she decided to let them know what her considerations were.

To her amazement, her fear and concerns were interpreted to mean that she was not committed to serving God. They told her that she was putting her job before God and that was a sin. So being a lover of God who didn't want to sin against God, she reluctantly picked a group to join as a member.

Her group met on Mondays and Thursdays between 7pm and 9pm. Belonging to a group automatically meant that she was a worker and as a rule, all workers were expected to be present for bible study meetings and mid-week services. The bible study meetings held on Tuesdays at 7pm while the mid-week services were for 6pm on Wednesdays.

Wanting to place God first and above her job, Mrs Foluke endeavoured to ensure that she didn't miss out on any of the meeting days. Mondays through Thursdays, she was in Church! She had little or no time for herself or her children but she consoled herself in that she was doing it all in service to God and that God was going to take care of her business.

Six months after she joined the group, she was awarded the "most committed" new member of the ministry. Soon after the award, she was told that the Lord had singled her out to serve in the prayer department. They told her God wanted to use her in the prayer group of the church. Meanwhile, the prayer group on the other hand met every Friday for an all-night vigil!

Now guess what! She wasn't even allowed to exempt herself from the first group. She was told that she didn't have to leave because there was no clash of meeting days or times! Literally, that meant that she became a full-time church staff. Going to church from Mondays to Fridays and keeping a demanding banking job.

In fact, we can safely say she was going to church from Sunday to Sunday because after her vigils on Fridays, she would be too tired to be useful to herself. She often spent her Saturdays sleeping and getting ready for Sunday's service.

This continued over a period of more than three years. While she was at it, her children began to keep bad company. Her teenage daughter often slept out and she didn't even know because she was busy "serving God". Her son began smoking, drinking and moving around with hooligans but she never knew.

She was too afraid to place anything before God that nothing else mattered to her. Not even the children God had given her. This continued until it began to affect her job. She started resuming late to work because she often overslept out of tiredness. When she wasn't late, she was found dozing off during working hours.

A woman who never received a query for more than the 15 years she had been working in the bank became a regular query recipient. First, it was one query in a month but soon grew to one a week. Severally, the management called her and warned her that if she wasn't going to change her ways, she was going to lose her job but all that fell on deaf ears because she didn't want to place anyone or anything ahead of God.

Expectedly, she showed up at work one day and receive the shock of her life. She was dismissed from work after almost 20 years of working in the bank. But that wasn't even the calamitous part of the story.

After she got fired, she went to church and reported to her leaders to see how they could help rally round her. Well, they told her that the devil was persecuting her for her faithfulness and devotion to God. And they were quick to assure her not to worry that the Lord would give her a better job. But it is well over ten years now since she lost that job and "the Lord" hasn't given her another one yet in quote!

Mrs. Foluke failed at raising her children like she should have. Those children ended up adding to the general national problem we are expecting God to take steps and solve today. She also succeeded in adding to the unemployment rate in Nigeria as well. All these because of the deception of religion and the gullibility of our people.

We are a group of people who will expect God to raise our children and probably do our jobs for us while they pray and fast, how can we then get involved with national transformation? Isn't it understandable why we will also need God to save our country for us?

If only in all our religious endeavours, we caught a glimpse of the mind of God our country will not be where it is today. If with all our zeal and passion, we knew exactly what God would have had us do, you will be surprised at what a nation we will be having today.

Only God can save Nigeria indeed – What a myth!

CHAPTER 2

Why God Is Not About To Save Nigeria

Why God Is Not About To Save Nigeria

If you have been following my line of discussion so far, you would have come to the conclusion that changing Nigeria is not entirely God's job. Therefore, no matter how long we wait for, "waiting on God" is not what is going to change the state of affairs in our beloved country. But just in case you are still not sure, let me show you something that will interest you from the scripture.

> *"Now unto him that is able to do exceeding abundantly above all that we ask or think, according to the power that worketh in us,"* (EPH 3:20)

Wow! What a great scripture we have here. No wonder we have several songs coined out of it already. But what gets my attention is the fact that in most cases, we only focus on the first part of this scripture. We often hear preachers preaching that "God is able to do exceeding abundantly above all that we can ask or imagine" They then go ahead to emphasize the fact that anything we can ask God for, He can do for us. They even tell us that anything we can think about or imagine God can do too. So all we have to do in life is think and ask and God swings into action performing and creating our thoughts and desires for us! Little wonder why we claim that only God can save Nigeria! But, how wrong this message is.

This is not a scripture where we have to look for another

verse of scripture from another book of the bible to get the full message. The very same verse itself says it all but we almost never take a second glance at the other part. No one ever tells us that even though God is able to do everything we can think about or ask for, the power to do everything you can ask or think about is not in heaven. The power to bring them to pass is not with God either. It is not even within the power of the angels of God to bring your requests and imaginations to pass.

The truth is this friends. While the bible states that God is able to do everything we can ask or think about, He will do them according to the power that works in us. It is in you and I that the power to bring these things to pass lies. It is in you and I that what it takes to make our desires and imaginations for our country come to pass lies. If we do nothing, it doesn't matter how many times we ask God or think about it, nothing will happen in our country. After we have prayed, we must avail God of ourselves to be used to bring the prayers to pass. God needs us to save Nigeria. He needs the power that is at work in our bodies otherwise, He cannot save Nigeria.

Therefore, instead of sitting and saying that only God can save Nigeria, we should start asking how we can become useful to God in saving Nigeria! We should find out how we can contribute our quota in God's salvation plan for Nigeria because until we all stand up and take our responsibility, I am sorry to say but nothing will happen!

LET'S SEPARATE TRUTH FROM MERE ASSUMPTIONS

As a journalist, one of the things I learnt was that the main point of a matter will always be hidden somewhere in the beginning of the story or towards the end of it. I find this to be true in relation to finding out God's plan and agenda for humanity.

When you read in the book of beginnings, right there in the first chapter, the bible elaborates on the process of creation from day one up until the seventh day on which God rested. We were told how that the lights were created. The firmaments after and then the waters were separated from the earth.

As soon as the earth (dry land) emerged, it was commanded to bring forth grass, the herb yielding seed, and the fruit tree yielding fruit after his kind, whose seed is in itself, upon the earth: and it was so. By the end of the fifth day, everything necessary for life on earth had been made. Then on the sixth day, God created His ultimate creature – man!

Just as He was about to do that though, He made a statement that encapsulates His purpose for man and the features that were going to be included in that man. Right there in the 26th verse of the 1st chapter, the bible tells us:

> "And God said, Let us make man in our image, after our likeness: and let them have dominion over the fish of the sea, and over the fowl of the air, and over the cattle, and over all the earth, and over every creeping thing that creepeth upon the earth." (GEN 1:26)

God made it clear that the man He wanted to create was one that would be in His image and likeness. This means that man was created to look like God and to function like God. The natural question I would ask then would be, why?

Why would God decide to create man to look like Himself and to function like Himself? Why wasn't it the birds of the air or the cattle of the field that were made to look like and function like Him? Why man instead? Of what importance is it to

God that man functions like Him? Hasn't He done enough for us by making us look like Him already? Why go the extra mile and make us function like Him?

In the answer to this question lies the true meaning of life for us as humans. But, thank goodness, we are not left to try to figure that out on our own. We are given a clear answer to this question and more right in the same book of Genesis.

> *"And God blessed them, and God said unto them, Be fruitful, and multiply, and replenish the earth, and subdue it: and have dominion over the fish of the sea, and over the fowl of the air, and over every living thing that moveth upon the earth."* (GEN 1:28)

Asides from telling us the reason for man and his features, as soon as man was created, God went on to elaborate on what he was created to do. God said he should be fruitful (productive), multiply (increase greatly), replenish the earth (restore to original level or condition). He also added that man should subdue the earth (bring under control) and to have dominion (reign as king over) the fish of the sea, the fowl of the air and over everything that moves upon the earth. So why should God be planning to come and save Nigeria when He has men there?

Man was placed in the earth to have dominion over all the three realms of existence in the earth. This is why God never had to invent the airplane, man did. God never had to invent a ship to move on the sea, man did. God didn't create cars and all the other vehicles that move on land, man did as well!

Friends, it is high time we stopped behaving like the creative ability of God was removed from Nigerians before they were born. We should stop acting like when God blessed man and said he should be fruitful, Nigerians were exempted!

How disheartening it is to know that someone has described our dear nation as a nation orchestrated to administrate and not to produce. Everyone is thinking of how to get elected into power so they can "be in control" Our country is full of so called engineers who only want to stay in air-conditioned offices. Youths no longer want to attend technical schools because it is now assumed to be less prestigious!

No one is thinking what they can do or produce for the benefit of the country yet, we have about 180 million people in whom God has placed His creative ability all living within the same country! And in the face of this, we have the courage to mouth our favourite lingo "only God can save Nigeria"

"My fellow Americans, ask not what your country can do for you, ask what you can do for your country" (JOHN F. KENNEDY)

My fellow Nigerians, let us stop asking and waiting for what our country can do for us. It is time we began to think of what we can do for our country. If the Wright Brothers can use their minds to subdue the forces of nature and build airplanes, we can use our minds to create a Nigeria that we will all admire. We can defy all odds and become a country orchestrated to produce and not just to administrate.

Over in the second chapter of the book of Genesis, God adds a little more details to man's job description.

"And the LORD God took the man, and put him into the garden of Eden to dress it and to keep it." (GEN 2:15)

This time around, God puts the same man whom he had told to be fruitful, multiply, replenish the earth, subdue it and have dominion over the three spheres of life; to dress and keep the garden. That makes it a 7-part responsibility God gave man at creation. Let's recall what they are for a moment:

1. Be fruitful
2. Multiply
3. Replenish the earth
4. Subdue the earth
5. Have dominion over the 3 spheres of life on the earth
6. Dress the earth
7. Keep the earth

Explaining each of these roles in detail one after the other would take me an entire book. But for the purpose of understanding what I am pointing out here, I will like to briefly explain something to you.

You will observe that every single responsibility God had in mind for which He created man in the first place was in connection to the earth. Everything He asked man to do for Him were things that had to be done on earth. So it would be right to say that man was originally created to take care of God's business here on earth.

This was the reason God had to make man in His image and likeness. He needed someone with His character who could perform like Him to take care of His business and creation on earth. He had no plan of being the one running the show on the earth otherwise He wouldn't have made man at all. So when the same man whom He made to take care of things on earth now turns over to Him and says "only God can save Nigeria" He becomes distraught and disappointed.

Imagine for a moment that you invested all your life's savings into buying up an estate. But since you were busy managing other affairs, you hired an estate manager whom you asked to take care of things around the estate. His job is to carry out your wish on that property and see to it that everything runs smoothly. But imagine that your estate manager doesn't do any of those. Instead he keeps bugging you with calls, SMS, emails and other available means of communication with requests that you should come and save the estate! He keeps telling everyone on the estate that only YOU can save the estate or solve the problems of the estate. What would you do? What would that mean to you?

That's exactly what it means to God when we persistently chant "only God can save Nigeria" While they are saying so, God is there wondering "of what use are you there in Nigeria if I still have to be the one to come and solve Nigeria's problems?" Aren't you supposed to be responsible for replenishing the earth? Aren't you there to dress and keep it?

Meanwhile, in case you are wondering what it even means to dress and keep the garden, let me expound it to you.

When God said man should dress the garden, He used a word that means to cultivate, work on, tend and care for it. He posits an idea that man was going to be responsible for the growth and development of things in the garden. He was charged to ensure that things never deteriorates in the garden. So you see why we cannot now turn around and say that only God can save Nigeria, all because it is our responsibility to save her.

The untold truth is that we have been created and factory fitted with all that we will ever need to cultivate the nation of Nigeria. We are the certified agents of change that have been placed here to see that the Nigerian dream comes to pass. We are the ones who have what it takes to work on Nigeria and bring about the desired growth and development in all the sectors of the nation. But when we neglect that role and responsibility that has been given us, we leave the country high and dry. We leave the future of the country in the hands of chance and guess where that lands us! In more trouble than we ever envisaged.

On the other hand, when God said to keep the garden, He meant that the man was to keep the earth in order, guard it, maintain it and watch over it. If anything ever went wrong with the earth, man was responsible for fixing it. At the same time, it was his role to ensure that he maintained and watched over the earth. So from any angle you view it from, the future and well-being of the earth was literally placed in man's hands and not God's hands.

It would therefore be unpardonable for anyone to turn around to then say that God is responsible for saving Nigeria. It is crystal clear that God has given that domain to man while He maintained His original domain in heaven.

> "The heaven, even the heavens, are the
> LORD's; But the earth He has given to
> the children of men." (Ps. 115:16)

This is another mind boggling revelation I must tell you. The religious folks will wish it was not in the bible but it's there. In fact, some of them will try to dismiss what is said here or give it a different interpretation but the message is clear.

Following the dialogue about what God had said all through the book of Genesis concerning man and his roles on earth, it should be clear what God meant in this portion of scripture. In simple terms, he was simply stating to us that territories have been marked. God in His infinite wisdom had decided to mark His territory and that of man.

He decided that He was going to be in charge of the heavens while man took care of things in the earth. He decided that having invested so much into creating and making man in His image and likeness, He could trust man to fully represent His interest in the earth. Therefore, he literally willed the earth to man. He made the earth man's area of influence and operation. He made the earth man's jurisdiction!

GOD IS WAITING ON US, NIGERIANS

Yes, it would be nice and cool for us all to sit back, fold our arms and sing that Jesus should take the wheels and reign over our dear country Nigeria. But guess what friends; that is not going to happen anytime soon. There is no amount of prayer we pray that is going to make Him "take control" like we often put it.

And in case you are wondering why this is so, it is because it is inconsistent with his nature and principles to do so. It is so inconsistent with His principles that back in the beginning, even after everything had been created spiritually, nothing really manifested physically until man was present there.

> *"These are the generations of the heavens and of the earth when they were created, in the day that the LORD God made the earth and the heavens, And every plant of the field before it was in the earth, and every herb of the field before it grew: for the LORD God had not caused it to rain upon the earth, and there was not a man to till the ground."* (GENESIS 2:4-5)

Notice that the bible says God created every plant of the field before it was in the earth and He made every herb of the field before it grew. We are then told that even though God had made these things, they never grew on the earth. That means potentially, these things were available but God was waiting for something!

Apparently, there were two very vital components necessary for these things to grow on the earth. One of them is the rain and the other is someone to till the ground. In other words, for the creations of God to perform normally in the earth, there has to be the rain (symbolizing the blessing of God) but most importantly, there has to be a man there. Until man was made, herbs couldn't grow. Until man was made, plants couldn't grow either. It was the man who made it possible for these things to begin to grow through his tilling of the ground.

Get this friends, while there might be a thousand and one things God might be willing to do and see happen in Nigeria, I am sorry to say that He would be incapacitated if there are no men in Nigeria. He would not be able to bring all those dreams and plans to pass no matter how many times we pray in a day or how many times we cry "oh God, come and take control"

The growth, development, stability and improvement we all crave for is in our hands. The future we all dream of and desire for our dear country is not about to come down from heaven. It is all within our reach right now. It is in our willingness to assume the responsibility that has been divinely committed to our trust as the managers and caretakers of the affairs of Nigeria.

Yes, you are the manager and caretaker of Nigeria. In the sphere of influence where God has placed you, He expects you to be responsible. He expects you to swing into action and bring about His plans there rather than sitting and chorusing "only God can save Nigeria"

It is time we began to call back our best hands that have fled the country in search of greener pastures. It is time our engineers returned home to invest their wisdom into the development of our motherland. It is time our experts and technicians came back home to face the responsibility that is before us a people. We need all the human resources we can possibly pool together now because that is the key to the national wealth and prosperity we all crave.

We can't have the literacy rate of our country at 50% in this age and time and be expecting that things will change. No wonder we all sit back waiting for God to come and do it. Come on here, is it God that will build our roads for us? Is it God that will build our hospitals? Or even if He builds the hospitals, will He also work there? Is it God that will build our schools and probably teach our children? Or maybe, we now need God to be our policeman and also preside over matters in our courts.

Fellow Nigerians, it is time we woke up from our slumber. It is time we took up the challenge and responsibility that is before us today. We are the ones to build our own country. We are the ones to build our own lives.

THE NIGERIAN HUMAN CAPITAL INDEX

Human Capital Index measures how well an organization or country makes use of the ability of an individual to perform and create value through his/her competencies, knowledge and expertise. It is a measure of how well the country puts the potentials of its citizens to use in producing national development and advancement. A higher human capital index indicates better management of human capital by the country. So where does Nigeria stand on the scale? What is our position in the world's record of human capital development?

According to the United Nations Development Program's Human Development Report released on the 14th of December 2015, all the countries of the world can be divided into 4 groups:

- Countries with very high human development
- Countries with high human development

- Countries with medium human development
- Countries with low human development

Would you like to guess where Nigeria falls on this list? I bet you wouldn't even make a mistake if you tried. Nigeria is right there on the list of countries with low human development. As a matter of fact, we are proudly number 152 in the world! Behind countries like Tanzania, Angola, Kenya, Swaziland, Gabon and even Botswana. What a record!

Then we turn around and say that only God can save Nigeria? We must be the biggest jokers around.

Dear Nigerians, it is time we upped our game as a nation. It is time we understood the value of the human resources that we have as a nation. It is time we began to enhance our human capacity as a country.

However, I don't want you to sit there and judge saying "see what the government has done." Don't sit there reading this and judging others for what has become our national cross to carry. Rather, I want you to think about how you can be instrumental to enhancing and developing our capacity as a nation. It all starts with taking responsibility for yourself and a few others within your own sphere of influence.

As much as lies within your capacity, make a commitment to seeing that those around you develop their expertise and competence and individuals while you do same. Do something to encourage the youths around you to go to school. Do something within your capacity to promote personal development in your own life as well as within your sphere of influence. When we all approach this as a common responsibility, I assure you that things will not remain the same in our country again.

As a nation, our problem is not a dearth of natural resources. There is hardly any state in Nigeria that doesn't have one natural resource or the other. We have natural resources. We have mineral resources but what we lack is human resources. That is why I advocate the development of our human capital as a country. We must take this seriously if we ever hope to build an enviable country for ourselves. And who is better positioned to do this other than you and me?

Therefore, let's stop this "only God can save Nigeria" madness and get to work building lives and indeed our country as a whole.

CHAPTER 3

The Earth Is Man's Jurisdiction

The Earth Is Man's Jurisdiction

Having established that God is not about to save Nigeria because He has men in place, let's take it a bit further as we look at the idea of the earth being man's jurisdiction and area of influence.

The word jurisdiction means the official power to make legal decisions and judgements. It refers to the area, territory or sphere of activity over which the legal authority of a court or other institution extends. So from the scriptural stand point of Psalm 115:16, we see that the earth is that territory within which man has the official power to make decisions and judgement. It is the realm over which man has been placed to preside and rule. Anything that goes wrong within that realm is the sole right and responsibility of man to fix.

Let's assume that there was a dispute between two individuals living in Lagos State for example. Let's call their names Mr. Kunle and Mr. Dayo. Also, let's assume that Mr. Kunle has a personal relationship with one of the judges of the International Court of Justice. So he decides to sue Mr. Dayo to the International Court of Justice. What do you think will happen? What do you think his judge friend will do?

It doesn't matter what level of relationship he has with that judge, the International Court of Justice cannot directly step into a case between two individuals living in the same state. Why? Because it is not within the jurisdiction of the court to do so. No matter how pained his judge of a friend might be about the case, he can't personally do anything about it. The best he can do is to find another judge with a court that has the jurisdiction to handle such a case.

Mr. Kunle can go around telling everyone that cares to listen that the International Court of Justice is going to intervene in the case between him and Mr. Dayo but that wouldn't change anything. He might even go to Mr. Dayo boasting and telling Him that he is going to deal with him at an international level but that still wouldn't move the needle. Not because the International Court of Justice is powerless but because the case at hand is way out of their jurisdiction!

This is exactly the same thing we do when we go chant our popular lingo "only God can save Nigeria" We are simply wasting time by thinking so because that is not God's jurisdiction. In fact, the only reason God will come to save Nigeria is when Nigeria becomes a country in heaven! But until that happens, it will be illegal for God to directly save Nigeria from heaven. This is where you come in!

You were created in the image and likeness of God so you could exercise authority over the earth. It is so that you can reign, dominate, rule, govern and have authority over the affairs of this world just as God has authority over the affairs of heaven. God placed you here to be an official representative of the kingdom of God. He placed you here as His care taker to protect His interest in this great nation. As a matter of fact, He made sure you were born a Nigerian because you are a carrier of a solution that Nigeria needs.

Understand that even though God rules in the affairs of men, the earth is not His jurisdiction. He only rules in the affairs of men either by the invitation of man or to save man from some self-inflicted dangers. Otherwise God indeed has relinquished the earth to the control of man.

From that scripture in the book of Psalms, we can see that the domain of God is primarily heaven. That is where He has limited himself to. He has chosen to make the heavens his jurisdiction while at the same time He himself makes it very clear that the earth has been given to man as man's sphere of influence. The earth is man's domain. Man therefore is responsible for what transpires here. You are responsible for what happens and what doesn't happen in Nigeria.

Therefore, we are supposed to create our own economy. We are supposed to create our own estate. If we want fast trains, we make them. If we want good roads, we make them. If we want a secured environment, we create it. Whatever it is we dream of as a nation, we simply swing into action and make it happen. I share steps on how to go about this in the second part of this book.

Did you ever hear or read of a country that was built because the people believed so much in God's ability to build their country for them? Even America that is described as God's own country did you ever hear that God actually came down to build and develop things for them? Of course not. They decided to make it what it is today and so can we. We can decide today that ours will no longer be a country known for corruption and hunger. Then we swing into action and deal with these problems that have eaten deep into the system of our nation like a malignant cancer.

GOD IS DOING A GREAT JOB TAKING CARE OF HIS BUSINESS

Yes, Yes and Yes! God is the owner of this world as much as He is the owner of heaven but guess what! He has relinquished his reigns and control over the affairs of this world and He has given it over to us. Such that if anything goes wrong in this world, God is not going to come down to fix it. Heavens no! That is not His responsibility; that is not His assignment. He has got His own roles and He is fulfilling them splendidly well. He is doing an outstanding job with His jurisdiction or will you like to contest that? Okay, here we go!

Have you ever heard that the sun refused to shine for one day in the part of the world that you are living in or in any part of the world for that matter? Have you ever heard, that the stars were falling out of heaven because there was a problem amongst the constellations of stars? Come on here, have you ever heard of a day that the moon fell out of the sky and the whole earth was plunged into total darkness? I bet you never heard something like that. Do you know the reason why you have never heard this before? It is because God is doing His own job of managing the Universe the best way possible.

God is responsible in His place of assignment, but the question is: are you responsible in your own place of assignment? Are you responsible in managing the affairs of this world that has been committed into the hands of the sons of men? Is it even a thought that hovers in your sub-consciousness that the earth is not within God's jurisdiction but within the ambit of man's operation? Or are you just sitting there saying "only God can save Nigeria?"

Do you know that this world has not been given into the hands of angels or the celestial beings but into your hand and the hands of your aunties, your brothers, sisters, friends, neighbours, cousins and every human being on earth?

Whatever happens to this world, whatever happens to the nations of the earth, whatever happens to our dear nation Nigeria is totally dependent on the reactions, responses and attitudes of the sons of men. We are the ones who are supposed to be managing the earth.

No wonder people cry and pray and ask God to come and take control of the affairs of this world yet it seems that there is never a response.

STOP CRYING OVER WHAT GOD HAS CREATED YOU TO FIX

When natural disasters occur, the Tsunami, epidemic of disease, heat wave, drought earthquake, floods, hurricane, terrorism attacks and all of those things that claim the lives in their thousands and millions, people cry out to God "Oh God, come and help us, come and save us, come and take control of this situation". But looking back in retrospect, in how many of those cases did you hear that God actually came down to save the situation? None. And what is the reason for that?

It is because while men were crying and calling on God to do something about a situation on earth, God in turn knowing fully well that He has handed the reigns and control of this world into the hands of men was waiting on man. He was waiting with a heavy heart for men to turn around and do something about the situation. And in those cases except a man stood up to the situation and faced it headlong, nothing got done.

For example, the case of Bill Gates who took it upon himself to eradicate polio totally from the face of the earth. He set about this mission using the vehicle of his foundation; Bill and Melinda Gates foundation. He partnered with the Global Polio Eradication Initiative made up of 4 spearheading organizations comprising of the World Health Organization (WHO), Rotary International, US Centers for Disease Control and Prevention (CDC), United Nations Children's Fund (UNICEF).

Together with several other partners, they have successfully reduced polio's outbreak by 99% and they are on course to eradicate it completely by the year 2018! As of now, polio has been totally eradicated from India where just barely few years ago they had the worst outbreak recording as much as 150,000 cases in a year.

Today, CDC Global Health reports that every country of the world is now polio free save for two – Pakistan and Afghanistan. However, the fight is still on-going to annihilate this disease completely from there as well.

To end the problem of child abuse in Nigeria, someone must arise. To end the problem of hunger and poverty in Nigeria, someone must arise from among us. To end the problem of Boko Haram, someone has got to arise with a strategy and plan to bring a permanent stop to their activities. We cannot afford to just sit down and pray while things keep deteriorating in our land.

Can you imagine that a man, just a single man like you is the one that took up that initiative to eradicate polio? What if he had also said "only God can save us from polio"? What if when the polio epidemic broke out and children were getting paralyzed and dying in their numbers, Bill Gates adopted the religious mindset of many Christians the world over today. What if he had also resorted to praying that God should take control of the situation? What do you think would be the situation in the world right now?

Millions of children would have been paralyzed by now and many more would have been dead. The situation must have gotten out of hand and the number of casualties would have been alarming. This is exactly, why the problems of Nigeria has lingered on for this long. When men were supposed to have taken action, they resorted to crying and calling out to God to come and save the situation. When we should have all taken our respective positions in the development of industries, the economy and the country as a whole, we were busy calling on God. We make it look as though God is retarded, wicked, indolent, and lazy. We make it look like God needs to be reminded of His duties through our prayers!

Oh sure lots of evidence abound to the fact that whereas people are supposed to be setting up work-stations in their offices, schools, homes, conference halls and so on across the nation; they would rather set up prayer stations! Whereas people should be deliberating, brainstorming, carrying out researches and planning out what they can do to turn around the tide of events in our nation, they would rather sit in churches crying and begging God to come and fix a problem that they have in their power to fix. How convenient!

This is quite unfortunate and it has got to stop because the earth has been given into the hands of the sons of men to manage it and fix it. Come on here friends, we are supposed to dictate the tune and pace of events in the affairs of the earth and that includes our beloved nation. We are supposed to look nature in the face and tell it, this is exactly what you should be doing. We are supposed to look the sea in the face and tell it what we want to do with it. We are supposed to look the forest in the face and tell it what we want to do with it. We are supposed to be planning and running the affairs of our world. We ought to take decisions over creation just as God rules over the Universe supremely. We should change our attitude and mindset and view everything that is created as being under us, under our power and subject to us.

WE ARE AS GODS OVER THIS WORLD

We should be aware of the tremendous power and authority that we have been given. The whole affairs of the world have been handed over to the ruler-ship of men. The whole affairs of the nations of the world have been committed to men of understanding, mighty men, and sons of God. As a matter of fact, God calls His children small gods. I mean gods in our essence and gods in our function, gods in the sense that we carry God's nature and we are born from God.

Every creation looks up to us as the gods of this earth, the animals, the plants, nature, the oceans, the seas and all look up to us as the gods of this world. So we ought to dominate them as gods and take decisions over this world.

Just for you to be clear on this, we are not elevating ourselves to the position of God Almighty but gods in relations to cow, cattle and over all of creation. It is imperative that I bring this to your attention. In some parts of India for example, people relate with cows and cattle and snakes as gods so they can't kill them or even touch them but it's supposed to be the other way round. We are the ones who have been made gods over cows, birds, animals, creation, seas, ocean, earthquake, and tsunami, name it. We are the ones who are supposed to reign and rule over them. We ought to dominate them as gods over them. And we ought to take over the decision making of this world.

When we see ourselves this way, we can then take up the challenge that we can make a difference in the world. We can actually begin to see that the answers we have been crying for all along have always been in our hands. The moment you adopt this mindset, you will discover that suddenly, you will start coming up with ideas for the transformation of your nation.

For crying out loud how many prayers do they pray in a country like Dubai for them to have witnessed the kind of rapid transformation they have witnessed in just about 20 years? Or how many night vigils do they hold in china for them to become the second largest economy after the United States? How many "fall and die" prayer do you hear being prayed in Japan for it to be among the largest economies in the whole world today? What about Saudi Arabia, India, Germany, France and all those nations who are economic superpowers? How religious are they and how close to God are they? How much do they value and honour the name of Jesus? Is it that they have two heads or what? Do you think they are the least bit better than we are as a people?

Wake up oh you sleeper, the authority to manage the earth and fix the problems of this world including the ones plaguing our great country Nigeria rests in your bosom. Stop waiting for God to come and save Nigeria because He really doesn't have to when you are there. The earth is your jurisdiction and area of influence, go ahead and be that influence God has made you to be.

CHAPTER 4

When God Moves, You Move!

When God Moves, You Move!

By now, you have a fair idea of the religious terrain in Nigeria. You understand that in as much as God is able to do exceeding abundantly above all we can ask or think for Nigeria, he can only do that to the measure of His power that is at work in us. He needs to use our physical bodies to bring His plans and purposes concerning Nigeria to pass because the earth is man's domain of influence and operation.

Now, it's time we went a little further in proving that the idea or school of thought that "Only God Can Save Nigeria" is nothing but a myth! It's only a statement born out of people's intention to abdicate their God-given roles and responsibilities. It is only a lie that has been so long in office that it is beginning to look like the truth. But, never mind because we are about to dethrone that idea from the minds of the Nigerian populace.

Something I'd like for you to know is the fact that our God is not a static being but rather, He is a multi-dimensional and a dynamic being. That is why in walking with Him, we must be careful to understand what He is saying now as opposed to what He said 50 years ago. We must be able to distinguish what He wants us to do now as opposed to what He wanted done several generations and dispensations ago.

For example, do you remember the journey of the Israelites when they travelled from Egypt into their promised land in the book of Exodus? Do you remember how long a journey it was and how God led them every bit of the way?

If you have an idea of what a wilderness looks like, then you will understand that it would have been practically impossible to journey through the wilderness and arrive at a desired destination without a form of map or guide. That explains why God had to lead them every step of the way with a physical sign of His presence.

They were not expected to take any step without God's leading. They were so spiritually insensitive to the leading of God that He had to lead them by physical signs. He had to appear to them as a pillar of fire at night and a pillar of cloud during the day. They had to follow the cloud every step of the way. When the cloud moved, they moved. Then, when it stopped, they stopped as well.

The majority of them had no idea what God's agenda for them as a nation was. They had no idea of where God was leading them neither did they have any clue as to who God was. Actually, they had no real relationship with God. They just followed as they were led by Moses and the cloud that was in their midst. Little or nothing was required of them in terms of taking the initiative. Even the laws they were given, they couldn't keep! All they knew to do was to sit pretty and wait for God to lead them.

It is rather unfortunate, that the church today has adopted this "Siddon look" mentality as well. We have been taught the "The LORD will fight for you; you need only to be still." message. We have been told that God is the one fighting the battles and we are just to stay calm while He deals with our enemies. This message has made the church so inactive that everything has been left in the hands of God.

Rather than taking action or taking the initiative, we have become so idle that other people now refer to Christianity as the religion for the lazy! They say that all that we Christians know how to do is to pray and hope for a miracle while others go ahead and make the records.

When confronted about our ineptness in taking action, we religiously say we are waiting for the leading of God. Whereas in reality, what we are saying is that God should do it Himself. God should fix things Himself. After all, that is why He is there – to fix stuff!

Now, let's make a close comparison between the Israelites at that time and the church today.

Did the Israelites have a personal relationship with God? No! Were the Israelites enabled to represent God to their world then? No! Did the Israelites know the will of God? No again! Why then should we expect the church that is on the complete opposite side to apply the same model and be successful? Why should we teach and train church people to "stand still and see the salvation of the Lord this day" when in reality, God didn't even approve of that when Moses said it?

STOP STANDING STILL TO SEE THE SALVATION OF THE LORD.

One of those teachings that the church has erroneously communicated to its people today is the one found in the book of Exodus. After the Israelites escaped from the land of Egypt and ran towards the direction of the red sea, it got to a point when they discovered that their oppressors wouldn't relent in their effort to keep them in bondage.

Lo and behold, the Egyptian army were after them and this time around, it was evident they weren't just coming to take them back as slaves. They were more likely to kill them than to capture them in order to enslave them.

Just like the popular prose, the Israelites were now trapped between the devil and the deep blue sea. Either way they turned, was disaster for them so they cried out to God for help. Haven experienced the miraculous power of God through the mighty signs he showed Pharaoh in the land of Egypt, they were probably hoping that God will send down fire from heaven to consume Pharaoh and his warriors. However, God was about to teach them their first lesson in the kingdom.

All the while that they were in the land of Egypt, God was the one doing everything in terms of getting them out. And here they were again, crying out unto Him for another miracle.

> *"And Moses said unto the people, Fear ye not,*
> *stand still, and see the salvation of the LORD,*
> *which he will shew to you to day: for the Egyptians*
> *whom ye have seen to day, ye shall see them again*
> *no more for ever. The LORD shall fight for you,*
> *and ye shall hold your peace."* (EXODUS 14:13-14)

Pastor Moses quickly told the people to relax and be still. He told them that they were going to see the salvation of the Lord that He would show them that day. He even added that the Egyptians they saw that day, they would never see again, forever.

You would think that God would be impressed that Moses was preaching such a message about His ability to save and deliver the people but let me surprise you friends. God wasn't impressed at all!

> *"And the LORD said unto Moses, Wherefore*
> *criest thou unto me? Speak unto the children*
> *of Israel, that they go forward:"* (EXODUS 14:15)

If there was any time when God told a man to shut up when he was busy praying, this was it. The bible says that God said to Moses, "why are you crying unto me" I mean God's answer to Moses' prayer that He should deal with the Egyptians they were seeing was "shut up Moses"

Instead of dealing with the Egyptians like they were expecting, God told Moses what they should do instead. He said "speak to the children of Israel that they go forward." Then He added another instruction for Moses and said:

> *"But lift thou up thy rod, and stretch out
> thine hand over the sea, and divide it: and
> the children of Israel shall go on dry ground
> through the midst of the sea."* (EXODUS 14:16)

Please pay close attention here …

I want you to notice that the request of Moses and the Is-raelites was for God to deal with their enemies. But God's an-swer was to show them what they were supposed to do. Do you remember what we saw in Eph 3:20 that God is able to do exceeding abundantly above all we ask or think?

God was able to do exactly what they wanted Him to do here but it was going to be according to His power that was at work in them. He required Moses to use the rod he had in his hand. He required Moses to stretch out that rod over the red sea and divide it!

Please also note that God didn't say "Moses, stretch out the rod you have in your hand and I will divide the red sea." Rather He said "Moses, you stretch out the rod in your hand and divide the red sea." In other words, God made the divid-ing of the red sea Moses' job rather than His. He showed us the dividing of the red sea was Moses' responsibility and not His.

Now imagine that Moses stayed there praying and fasting and asking God to divide the same red sea that was in his ca-pacity to divide. Imagine that Moses stood there telling the Israelites that only God can save them. What do you think would have happened that day?

The Egyptians would have caught up with them and killed every single one of them. Then the religious folks would have said "the Israelites were such a religious group, they died calling on God" or "they died standing still and waiting for the salvation of the Lord"

Oh, how many sectors of the economy of our nation have degenerated and even died because we have been standing still and waiting for the salvation of the Lord? Some of us who should have taken certain actions or steps to move our country forward have been calling on the name of the Lord rather than doing what God has already enabled us to do. That is why our beloved country is in the mess it is today.

I wonder how many of our prayers God has been answering with the same answer He gave Moses that day. I wonder how many times we have gathered in our multitudes to pray to God and asked Him to come and save Nigeria and His answer was "will you all shut up and go do something!" or "will you all get out there and take charge of things like I have enabled you to?"

It is time we came out of the school of thought that only God can save Nigeria. It is time we began to take the necessary steps to deliver our country from the hands of corruption and destruction. Now is the time to take the bull by the horns and start doing things to turn our country into the dream and plan of God Almighty.

Of what use will the investment of God into the church be if He still has to be responsible for everything? Of what good is our knowledge of the will of God if God will still be responsible for their fulfilment? Or maybe we are not even sure what the will of God is for Nigeria.

How can God still be responsible for saving Nigeria when He has saved more than 80 million of her citizens? How can God be responsible for a country where He has more than 80 million children? How can God be responsible for changing a country that is acclaimed to have the highest attendance to church services? A whopping 89% attendance when even the United States that is called God's own country only has about

44% attendance rate? Something is definitely not right with our understanding of Christianity and church. Something is definitely not correct with our theology and now is the time for a change.

IT'S TIME TO START USING OUR GENIUSES

"God and Nature first made us what we are, and then out of our own created genius we make ourselves what we want to be. Follow always that great law. Let the sky and God be our limit and Eternity our measurement." (MARCUS GARVEY)

I couldn't agree more with the words of Marcus Garvey here. While we are busy hoping, praying, fasting and expecting God to save Nigeria, God is busy waiting for us to put His investments into us to good use!

Do you have an idea of how many great things a few Nigerians have accomplished over the years? Do you know how many Nigerians have received international recognition for something they did outstandingly well? Do you know what great feats Nigerians are accomplishing all over the world? Here are just a few of them for you:

Ahmadu Bello (Knight of the British Empire)

Sir Ahmadu Bello KBE (June 12, 1910 - January 15, 1966) was a Nigerian politician who was the first and only premier of the Northern Nigeria region. He also held the title of Sardauna of Sokoto. Bello and Abubakar Tafawa Balewa were major figures in Northern Nigeria pre-independence politics and both men played major roles in negotiations about the region's place in an independent Nigeria. As leader of the Northern People's Congress, he was a dominant personality in Nigerian politics throughout the early Nigerian Federation and the First Nigerian Republic.

Bello was made a Knight of the British Empire (KBE) by Queen Elizabeth II of England in 1959.

Abubakar Tafawa Balewa (Knight Commander of the Order of the British Empire)

Alhaji Sir Abubakar Tafawa Balewa, KBE (December 1912 - January 15, 1966) was a Nigerian politician from Bauchi, and the only prime minister of an independent Nigeria. Originally a trained teacher, he became a vocal leader for Northern interest as one of the few educated Nigerians of his time. He was also an international statesman, widely respected across the African continent as one of the leaders who encouraged the formation of the Organization of African Unity (OAU). Nicknamed the Golden Voice of Africa because of his oratory, he stands out as one of the only three National Heroes of the Nigerian Nation.

In January 1960, Balewa was knighted by Elizabeth II as a Knight Commander of the Order of the British Empire (KBE). He was awarded an honorary doctorate from the University of Sheffield in May, 1960.

In 1957, Balewa was appointed Chief Minister, forming a coalition government between the NPC and the National Council of Nigeria and the Cameroons (NCNC), led by Nnamdi Azikiwe. He retained the post as Prime Minister when Nigeria gained independence in 1960, and was re-elected in 1964.

He was overthrown and murdered in a military coup on January 15, 1966, as were many other leaders, including his old companion, Ahmadu Bello. Today, his portrait adorns the

ONLY GOD CAN SAVE NIGERIA: WHAT A MYTH!

five Naira Note. The Abubakar Tafawa Balewa University in Bauchi is named in his honour.

Abubakar Gumi (King Faisal International Prize)

Abubakar Gumi (COFR) (1922-1992) was an outspoken radical Islamic scholar and Grand Khadi of the Northern Region of Nigeria (1962-1967), a position which made him a central authority in the interpretation of the Sharia legal system in the region. He was a close associate of Ahmadu Bello, the premier of the region in the 1950s and 1960s and became the Grand Khadi partly as a result of his friendship with the premier. In 1967, the position was abolished.

Apart from his national award, he received the King Faisal International Prize from Saudi Arabia for his translation of the Quran into Hausa language.

At a time in his political career, after his closest political ally, Sir Ahmadu Bello and Sardauna of Sokoto had exited finally by the January, 1966 coup that brought the First Republic to an abrupt end, he became a supporter of women's rights to vote.

Wole Soyinka (Nobel Prize for Literature)

Akinwande Oluwole Babatunde Soyinka (born 13 July, 1934), popularly called Wole Soyinka is a Nigerian playwright and poet. He was awarded the 1986 Nobel Prize in Literature, the first and so far the only Nigerian to be honoured in that category.

After his studies in Nigeria and the UK where he bagged his BA in Literature at the University of Leeds, he worked with the Royal Court Theatre in London. He went on to write plays that were produced in both countries, in theatres and on radio. He took an active role in Nigeria's political history and its struggle for independence from Great Britain.

Soyinka was awarded the Nobel Prize for Literature in 1986, becoming the first Nigerian laureate. He was described as one "who in a wide cultural perspective and with poetic overtones fashions the drama of existence".

Philip Emeagwali (Gordon Bell Prize winner)

Philip Emeagwali (born in 1954) is an Igbo Nigerian-born engineer and computer scientist/geologist who was one of two winners of the 1989 Gordon Bell Prize, a prize from the Institute of Electrical and Electronic Engineers (IEEE), for his use of a Connection Machine supercomputer to help analyse petroleum fields. He performed the world's fastest calculation at 3.1 billion calculations per second.

This calculation was remarkable not only because it was twice as fast as the previous world record, but also because of the method used to achieve this phenomenal task. Rather than use a multimillion dollar supercomputer, Emeagwali used the Internet to access 65,536 small computers simultaneously (called massively parallel computers).

This technology is revolutionising the oil industry as it is used to help simulate how to recover oil from oilfields, thus helping oil producing nations to efficiently extract more oil and increase their oil revenues. It is also applicable to the field of meteorology as it can be used to help predict weather patterns for the next 100 years forecast.

Nwankwo Kanu (Olympic Football Gold Medalist)

Nwankwo Kanu (born 1 August, 1976), popularly called Papilo, perhaps owing to his willowy physique, is a retired Nigerian footballer of Igbo extraction who played as a forward. Kanu's magnum opus was his leading Nigeria's U-23 football team (otherwise referred to Dream Team I) to victory at the 1996 summer Olympics thereby becoming the winner of the

Olympic soccer gold medal of that year. He was a member of, and later captained, the Nigerian national team, the Super Eagles, for 16 years from 1994.

Kanu's international success includes a FIFA under-17 World Cup title in 1993 and the 1996 Olympic football gold medal, UEFA Champions League medal among several others. He is also a UNICEF Goodwill Ambassador.

He announced his retirement from international football at the 2010 World Cup in South Africa.

The 1996 Summer Olympics were a summer multi-sport event held in Atlanta, Georgia, United States from 19 July to 4 August 1996. A total of 10,318 athletes from 197 National Olympic Committees (NOCs) competed in 271 events in 26 sports.

Chioma Ajunwa (Olympic Gold Medalist)

Chioma Ajunwa-Opara, popularly known as Chioma Ajunwa, is a Nigerian former athlete who specialised in the long jump. Ajunwa hails from Ahiazu Mbaise in Imo State. After various setbacks in her career, she achieved fame when she became the first athlete in her country to win an Olympic gold medal at the 1996 Summer Olympics in Atlanta, and to date remains Nigeria's only individual Olympic gold medalist. Ajunwa is also an officer with the Nigerian Police Force.

As a professional sportswoman, Ajunwa originally played football for the Nigerian women's team and was a member of The Falcons during the Women's World Cup in 1991.

Ajunwa performed as a track and field athlete and specialised in 100m, 200m and long jump, eventually competing at the African Championships in 1989 and the All Africa Games in 1991 where she won the gold medals in the long jump.

Agbani Darego (Miss World)

Ibiagbanidokibubo 'Agbani' Asenite Darego, popularly called Agbani Darego, (born December 22, 1982) is a model, best known as the first black African to be crowned Miss World in 2001. Darego hails from Abonnema, Rivers, and was born into a family of eight children.

Darego managed to divide her time between her education at the University of Port Harcourt where she was studying Computer Science, and representing Nigeria in the 2001 Miss Universe competition, held in Bayamón, Puerto Rico. She was placed among the top 10 semi-finalists, finishing seventh. She was the only black semi-finalist that year - and the only finalist to wear a maillot swimsuit. In November 2001, Darego was crowned Miss World, beating Miss Scotland and Miss Aruba in the final round.

Chimamanda Ngozi Adichie
(Commomwealth Writers' Prize for Best
Book/ Orange Prize for Fiction)

Chimamanda Ngozi Adichie (born September 15, 1977) is a writer whose first two novels won literary awards. She is a native of Abba, in Njikoka Local Government Area of Anambra State. At the age of 19, Adichie left Nigeria and moved to the United States for college and studied at Drexel University in Philadelphia. In 2003, she completed a master's degree in creative writing at Johns Hopkins University in Baltimore. In 2008, she received a Master of Arts in African studies at Yale University. Chimamanda is a 2008 MacArthur Fellow.

Her first novel, Purple Hibiscus, was published in 2003 and won the 2005 Commonwealth Writers' Prize for Best First Book. Her second novel, Half of a Yellow Sun, named after the flag of the short-lived Biafran nation, is set before and during the Biafran War. It was published by Fourth Estate in the UK and by Knopf/Anchor in 2006 and was awarded the 2007 Orange Prize for Fiction.

Mike Adenuga (African Entrepreneur of the Year)

Michael Adeniyi Agbolade Ishola Adenuga Jr (born 29 April 1953), popularly called Mike Adenuga, is a Nigerian business tycoon, and the second richest person in Nigeria. His company, Globacom is Nigeria's second-largest telecom operator, and also has a presence in Ghana and Benin. He also owns stakes in the Equitorial Trust Bank and the oil exploration firm, Conoil (formerly Consolidated Oil Company). Forbes has estimated his net worth at $3.2 billion as of September 2015 which makes him the second wealthiest Nigerian behind Aliko Dangote, and the sixth richest person in Africa

In August of 2007, Adenuga was named the African Telecoms Entrepreneur of the Year for his courageous and rapid investment in the telecom sector. The recognition was given at the 2007 maiden Africa Telecoms Award event held in Lagos and witnessed by prominent Africans.

Oluwatoyosi Ogunseye (Knight International Journalism Award)

Who says there are no competent journalists of international standards in Nigeria?

Oluwatoyosi Ogunseye, a Mandela Washington Fellow from Nigeria, recently received the 2014 Knight International Journalism Award by the United States-based International Centre for Journalism (ICFJ). This prestigious award recognises outstanding investigative journalistic ability that makes a difference in the lives of people around the world.

Her stories are not just award-winning -- they have catalysed positive change. In one of such, she published a piece on infant mortality rates at a top hospital in Lagos that pressured the hospital to purchase more incubators for high-risk new-borns.

Recently, March 9, 2016 to be precise, she received the Presidential Precinct's inaugural Young Leader Award.

The Presidential Precinct, which announced the creation of the Young leader Award in January 2016 presented her with it in Charlottesville, Virginia.

Ogunseye is a two-time winner of the CNN/Multichoice African Journalists Award and several other national and international awards.

Aliko Dangote (African Person of the Year)

Aliko Dangote GCON (born 10 April 1957) is a Nigerian billionaire, who owns the Dangote Group. The company operates in Nigeria and other African countries, including Benin, Ethiopia, Senegal, Cameroon, Ghana, South Africa, Togo, Tanzania, and Zambia. As of January 2015, he had an estimated net worth of US$18.6 billion.

Dangote was named as the Forbes Africa Person of the Year 2014. In 2013, Alhaji Dangote and six other prominent Nigerians were conferred Honorary Citizenship of Arkansas State by Governor Mike Beebe who also proclaimed May 30 of every year as Nigeria Day in the US.

Oba Otudeko (Africa CEO of the Year)

Ayoola Oba Otudeko, CFR (born, August 18, 1943) is a Nigerian investor and entrepreneur whose domestic and foreign interests cut across diverse sectors of the economy. The Nigerian business mogul, who is the chairman of Honeywell Group beat seven other finalists, including Africa's richest man, Aliko Dangote, to clinch the coveted prize of Africa Chief Executive (CEO) of the Year (2016) at a meeting of more than 800 chief executives across the continent held in Abidjan, the capital of Cote d'Ivoire.

Set up in partnership with the AFDB, the Africa CEO Forum is an event organized jointly by Groupe Jeune Afrique, publisher of Jeune Afrique and The Africa Report, and Rainbow Unlimited, a Swiss company specializing in organizing economic promotion events

How can someone now look at a country with these caliber of men and women and conclude that we do not have what it takes to fix our problems? How dare we resort to the piteous monologue that "only God can save Nigeria"?

Dear Friends, it's time we all stood up to the challenge before us and bring out the best in us to make our country the hub of progress and development that it was designed to be. It's time we forgot the idea of waiting on God to come and fix our roads, curb the corruption, build our schools, create jobs and so on. We must now take our national destiny into our hands and chart a course for growth and development in our country.

PART 2

Challenging the
Church of the Day!

CHAPTER 5

Re-educating the Church

Re-educating the Church

Congratulations on making it thus far in this book. If you are still here, then you are the real deal. You are ready to learn the exact steps it will take for us as a nation to leave the "only God can save Nigeria bandwagon" and jump on the "let's save Nigeria bandwagon"

But first, we must begin by re-educating the church! Yes, it is a fact that the heroic men and women of faith that have served God in our country over these years have done a great job. They have done commendably well in gaining some ground and reclaiming territories for our God and master. However, the truth remains that there is still a lot more to be done. There is a lot that we still have to accomplish out there in the world. There are much more territories to be taken over for God than we have already taken.

This is why the church must rise and take up the challenge and responsibility that we have before us in this day and time. The church must take its place as the pillar and foundation of truth. It must change from a place for grooming people who only seek after the hand of God to those who seek after His heart.

For us to have the Nigeria of our dreams, the church must rise up to the occasion and begin to train its members into Sons of God. It must change its message from being man-centered to God centered. People should begin to find God in our churches rather than just getting the things they need for daily existence. We (Pastors and church leaders) have to train the people to stop using God for their selfish needs and begin to avail themselves to be used of God.

We must understand that even though God has created and

put all humans on earth to dominate and take care here, the church is still His first choice. But then, the church has not been effective in representing the mind and will of God in our nation because it has been wrongly taught over the years. We have been taught that Christianity is all about attending services and giving offerings. We have been taught that being a follower of Christ is all about doing good works and making sure you are not sinning. In fact in some cases, the church has focused its message on the deliverance of the same people for whom Jesus died.

No wonder things have been increasingly deteriorating in our nation despite our strong religious affiliation. While we have been going to church and playing holy, things have moved from bad to worse and even worst in the land. And sadly, we haven't even noticed that something is wrong with our strategy and modus operandi.

From generation to generation, we have applied the same formula. The same strategy that our forefathers applied without much results are the same strategies we have been applying. Or should I say we have even applied worse ones today. We cry that things aren't going on well in the land yet we preach that politics is a dirty game that should not be dabbled into by Christians. When some dare to go ahead to participate in politics, we label them rebels. We call them backsliders and literally separate them from the rest of us who are too holy to play dirty.

Yet, year in year out, we pray for the government. We pray for things to change but never think God would use us to effect that change. Sometimes, it feels like we are just expecting that by praying, God will just swing a magic wand and turn everything around in our country. We seem not to have understood the fact that God always needs a man to perform His will here on earth.

The climax of it all is that some even go as far as praying for God to kill all the bad eggs in the society. Some have said that they wished it were possible to gather all the bad politicians in one place at the same time and just blow the place up. Or better still manage to get all of them on an airplane and just crash the plane. We just spend energies and initiatives that should have been used to foster growth and increase in the country to plan the downfall of those we think have led us badly.

These and more are the reasons why I hold the opinion that the church must be re-educated. We need to be told what the truth of the kingdom really is. We need to become acquainted with the ideals of the kingdom of God. We must learn the true meaning of the fact that we are the light of the world and the salt of the earth.

YOU ARE THE SALT OF THE EARTH

"Ye are the salt of the earth: but if the salt have lost his savour, wherewith shall it be salted? it is thenceforth good for nothing, but to be cast out, and to be trodden under foot of men." (MATT 5:13)

Sometimes I wonder if scriptures like this are not being included in the bibles that are shipped to Nigeria. Or maybe that portion has been torn out of the Nigerian's Christian bibles!

For goodness sake, how can we read scriptures like this and still be comfortable sitting down in pews and doing nothing to take over our nation for God? How can we hear that we are the salt of the earth and still turn around to say that "only God can save Nigeria"? Did you ever read that God is the salt of Nigeria? Did you ever read that the angels are the salt of Nigeria? How can those of us who have been told that we are the salt neglect our roles all in the name of prayer?

Among other things, three functions of salt that I like to bring to your notice are the fact that salt is used to flavour, to preserve food and as a source of nutrient.

1.   Flavour:

Salt acts in multiple ways to enhance the flavour of food. Not only is the "salty" flavour element one of the most desired by humans, but salt can also affect other flavor elements, such as sweet and bitter.

In small amounts, salt will intensify sweetness and is therefore often sprinkled on fresh fruit or added to candies like caramel. Salt can also counteract bitter flavours in food. For this reason salt is often used to "de-bitter" cruciferous vegetables and olives.

With that in mind, imagine what might have been on God's mind when He said you are the salt of the earth. Why will you be in a local government, city, state or a country as a whole and the place has no flavor? Why will you work somewhere and the place has no flavor? It must mean that you have lost your savor as a child of God and guess what, that spells doom for that place.

2.   Preservative:

Another very important function of salt is in the preservation of food items. Salt curing meat and other foods is the oldest method of food preservation and was was heavily used prior to refrigeration. Salt acts as a preservative by drawing out moisture from food, which is essential to microbial growth. Many pathogenic microbes are also simply unable to grow in the presence of salt.

Does this now ring a bell in your heart about you being the salt of the earth? Can you imagine what a country we will have if just half of the believers there would become preservatives in the society? Think of how many micro-bial growths (problems facing our country today) will find it impossible to grow because of our preservative function! Think of how many problems facing the country will be inhibited just by our being the salt of the land!

Now, imagine what a sight it is for the same salt that should have been the preservative of the land to be crying out saying "only God can save Nigeria" To put it mildly is to call it disastrous!

But then, it's the church I blame. It's the leadership of the church that we should question because they have obviously done a bad job in educating their members. The members who should have discovered God for themselves in our church services have only learnt how to use God. People who should have been growing in the knowledge of God are growing in the doctrines and philosophies of men instead.

Believers who should have been trained and taught to go into the various sectors of the country and be the salt of the earth have been restricted to pews. They have been taught that all that matters is attendance to church services while the environment where the services hold stay in absolute darkness and degradation.

We must now set out to be the preservative force that God has made us. We must preserve the beauties of our culture.

3.   Nutrition:

Last but in no way the least is nutrition. Although most people consume far too much sodium, it is a nutrient essential for human survival.

Pure table salt is comprised of approximately 40% sodium and 60% chlorine. Most table salts also have iodine added to them to prevent iodine deficiencies. Iodine deficiencies can cause disorders of the thyroid, including goiters.

God must mean that we are responsible for the health and well-being of our dear nation Nigeria. The church is the one that is supposed to bring about the healthy society we are dreaming about. The church is supposed to be the catalyst for the growth that we all wish and pray for. But all these will never happen when the salt has lost its savor. All these will never happen when the salt decides to sit back and wait for God to come and save Nigeria.

Something that bothers me even the more about this condition the church has found herself is the statement Jesus made about the salt that has lost its savour. In His words, He said if the salt has lost its savour, it is therefore good for nothing!

Oh how many millions of people who should have been busy adding flavour to our country, preserving the country and nourishing it have become good for nothing? Countless number of us have literally become useless in the affairs of the land thereby leaving the country in the hands of the likes of Boko Haram and co. People who ordinarily should sit and let us lead and show them how to run the country have taken the reigns of the country because the sons of God have lost their savour.

Dear friends, God is calling for a change right now. Dear Pastors, God is calling for a change that will begin from our pulpits. He is asking that we begin to re-educate the church in Nigeria. We must begin to show them who they really are in Christ and what they can do. We must let them know that the reason things have remained the way they have remained all these while is because they haven't been involved with the system.

We must train the church to stop the fear of being involved

with the politics of the land. We must re-indoctrinate them against the idea that politics is a dirty game that should only be played by the dirty.

Dear Pastors, it's time to start pushing people of the pews into their various fields and strata of the society. It's not enough to send people out to the streets to evangelize and bring in more people to church. We must begin to send people out to dominate every sphere of influence out there. Every church has got to draw a plan and strategy to completely take over its immediate environment.

Stop holding all night prayers asking God to take control. Start training people to take over the various spheres of the society. Let's make our churches centers for the development and training of national transformers. Stop joining them to say that "only God can save Nigeria" because God wouldn't need to come down to change things when He has us there.

GOD DOESN'T HAVE TO DO IT WHEN YOU ARE THERE

I remember the inspiring story of our very own Arch Bishop Benson Idahosa. In his report of the incidence, he wrote:

Several years ago, all the witches in the world met in Chicago, and at that meeting, they took a decision to hold their first world conference in Africa. And do you know exactly where they decided the meeting should be held? My city: Benin-City, Nigeria!

Their chief host held a press conference, granted our media network an interview and informed them with pride that the first universal conference of witches and wizards would be held in Benin City. When they told me, I said what? They said a world conference of witches. I asked where? They said, in Benin-City, my city where I live!

I told them that it could not be true because it was NOT possible. Shout Hallelujah! If I be a man of God! It was not possible, it was not true, could not be true! The press asked what was not possible? I told them that witches from the world over could not come to Benin-City. Then they asked what I would do to them if they came. I answered that I would kill them all.

They then called on the proposed chief host and told him, "Dr. Benson Idahosa says your world conference of witches cannot hold in Benin-City."

Responding he said, "Not even God can stop it."

He boasted that he was a wizard, and he knew their power.

Our national dailies carried this information on their front pages to the effect that the chief host of Witches and Wizards conference says not even God could stop the conference! The press hurried to me to report that the chief host had said not even God could stop it.

I said he was correct. They said what? I told them that God did not need to waste His time stopping witches from coming to Benin-City for a conference. "That is why I am here. The Lord does not need to consider matters as trivial as the stopping of the conference of witches."

In an interview several years later, his wife – Bishop Margret Idahosa said she recalled her fear for his life when he confronted the witches in Benin. She was so scared for his life but he would always tell her to be at the same pace with him. He always told her that he wanted her to be on the same terrain with him and see what God will do.

The late Archbishop went on air and said there was no way they could hold a meeting where he was, declaring the meeting would not hold. And true to his words, the meeting didn't hold even when the chief priest had threatened that it would. After that encounter, my faith in God was further strengthened."

Wow, what a story. What a man!

He said the Lord does not need to consider matters as trivial as stopping a conference of witches because he was in that city. Can you say that the Lord doesn't have to consider trivial things because you are here today? Can you say that the Lord doesn't have to bother Himself with what is going on in the educational sector of the country because you are there? What about the banking and finance sector? Can it be said that God doesn't have to consider that because you are there? What area of life are you taking care of as a person? In what areas of life does the Lord not have to bother because you are there?

Bishop Margret Idahosa added that in another instance in the life of Arch Bishop Benson Idahosa, the Oba of Benin died and there was an order that every man in Benin should shave his head. The Arch Bishop not only defied the order, he also instructed members of the church not to comply because there was no way the living should shave their heads for the dead, adding that we grow our hair for the living.

At that point, she was so scared for his safety and life, but she trusted God to help him in those trying times because of his unwavering belief in God. The royal family was not happy with him, they did the burial ceremony of the Oba for seven days and pronounced death on those who did not comply with the directive, particularly the Arch Bishop. They gave him seven days to live, but he did not die. He only died when God said it was time for him to leave the scene and that was many years after the incident!

Talk about someone who knew who he was in Christ. He lived to the fullest as the salt of the earth and his environment in particular. The question is, where then are the believers of like mind today? Where are believers who can defy all odds to represent God and His kingdom? It is those kinds of sons that our nation needs to arise right now. It is those who can stand for God in the face of oppositions and threats. It is those who can stand in the face of threats of death that can really bring that change we all crave to our country.

You who are reading this now, I want you to know that as an individual, you are a salt that has been sent to Nigeria. It is not a mistake that you are a Nigerian. It is not a mistake that God brought you into this part of the world. It is definitely because He has put the answer to at least one of the myriads of problems facing Nigeria in you. And my goal with this book is to stir you to action. My dream is to get you up and running dishing out that solution that is inside you for the improvement and development of our motherland. Please do not join those who claim that only God can save Nigeria. Do not resign to fate and inactivity in the guise that Nigeria's problems are too acute for anyone including yourself handle.

In the next part of this book, I will be showing you how simple individuals have applied the same model I am going to be sharing with you to bring about tremendous change in their country. Then I will show you how you can apply the same beginning from where you are. It is my conviction that if you apply this model, while others will be waiting for God to come and save Nigeria, you would be making tremendous progress as the salt of the earth in Nigeria.

CHAPTER 6

Exploits Of the Heroes of Faith

Exploits Of the Heroes of Faith

In opening this chapter, to say that the contemporary church has not been very effective in championing the cause of national development is to put it mildly. However, there are certain "old faith heroes" who achieved significant things in the early days of the church in Nigeria whom I wouldn't fail to mention.

These are faithful servants of God who went out of their way to do things worthy of mention. Certain men and women who did outstandingly well in their time; laying down their lives for the growth of the church. Some of them you will get to meet in this chapter.

I would love to point out some of the things they did that made them stand out in their days. It is my firm belief that doing this will enable this generation of believers (ministers and congregants alike) understand where the church has been and how we can better take her forward. It is also my desire that the exemplary acts of these faithfuls that are chronicled here will be emulated by this current church age.

1.   Samuel Ajayi Crowther (1808 to 1891):

Crowther was born with the name Ajayi in Osogun, in the Egba section of the Yoruba people, in what is now known as western Nigeria. When he was about 13, he was taken as a slave by Fulani and Yoruba Muslim raiders and sold several times before being purchased by Portuguese traders for the transatlantic market. His ship was intercepted by the British navy's anti-slave trade patrol, and the slaves were liberated in

Sierra Leone.

There he was educated by the Church Missionary Society (CMS), became a Christian, and was baptised; taking at baptism the name of an eminent clergyman in England, Samuel Crowther. Following a brief visit to England he enrolled in the Fourah Bay Institute, and after graduating became a school teacher.

He impressed his superiors as intelligent and very devout, and was invited to join the British Niger Expedition (1841). He then went to England where he was ordained (1845). He returned to West Africa as a missionary, serving briefly at Badagry before being posted to Abeokuta in Yorubaland (1846). He was the first African bishop of the Anglican church; explorer and missionary in southern Nigeria.

Thoroughly Victorian in his outlook, he was immensely successful in promoting Christianity, missionary education, and capitalistic development throughout the Niger valley.

WHO IS A MISSIONARY?

For many of us, a missionary is simply someone who goes about preaching the gospel and all that. While that is true, we must understand a whole new dimension of what it means to be a missionary. Yes there are some who will have to be sent into places to preach the gospel. But the truth remains that everyone of us is a missionary in our own way.

Whatever field of endeavour or sphere of life you are connected to is your mission field. Any problem you have identified that you are equipped to solve is your mission field. The solution you have been packaged to deliver to the world is your mission field my friend.

So as a church, it is high time we began to teach the people that they are all missionaries. In fact, part of the assignments we have to every individual is to help them discover their mission field. No one should be allowed in our churches to just come and sit down. No one should be allowed to just be a church member without having a real mission field out there where they are taking the kingdom to.

In fact, if we must use the term membership in church, we should never measure membership by how many people gather to listen to us on Sundays but by how many people we have helped to become real missionaries taking territories for the Lord. Churches must begin to measure success by how many they reach through the mission fields rather than how many they gather every Sunday.

Imagine that because of Samuel Ajayi Crowther that returned to the country with a mission, there is such a thing as the Anglican church in Nigeria today. I mean more than 100 years after the death of the man, what he brought to Nigeria is still living and active. How much more can we do if only half of the people who gathered in our cathedrals on Sundays took up their own mission fields and excelled there?

THE "THREE-SELF" CHURCH MODEL

The CMS secretary, Henry Venn, saw Crowther as a potential demonstration of the feasibility of self-governing, self-supporting, and self-propagating African churches and in 1857 sent him to open a new mission on the Niger. The entire staff was African, mainly from Sierra Leone, and Venn moved toward an Anglican version of the "three-self" formula by securing Crowther's appointment in 1864 as "Bishop of the countries of Western Africa beyond the Queen's dominions."

I like for you to take notice of what I refer to as the three-self church model here. It was a self-governing, self-supporting and self-propagating church!

Unfortunately, what we have in our churches today are far from that. They are far from being self-governing, self-supporting or even self-propagating. We have churches in Kogi state that cannot function independent of the "headquarters" in Lagos state. We have churches in Uyo today that send every bit of money that comes into their coffers to some headquarters somewhere else. Later we begin to wonder why the churches aren't effective in changing their communities. We wonder at why we have churches that are no more than just a gathering of people.

What the missionaries brought was a church model that ensured the church could govern, support and propagate itself. And that is the true definition of a living church my friends. When a church needs permission from "headquarters" to meet the needs of its people then something is fundamentally wrong. When church people have to write series and series of letters to the HQ just to have dates approved for their baby dedications, wedding ceremonies and other concerns they might have, something is really wrong.

Such churches cannot be effective in their immediate environment and as such will have no place in terms of national transformation. The time has come for us to go back to the old good model that worked and is still working till date. This model is what enabled the missionaries of old to take up sectors in the economy and fund projects without waiting on the government.

THE AJAYI CROWTHER LEGACY

Although Crowther is best remembered for his missionary activities, he also made valuable scholarly contributions in his journals of the Niger expeditions, and his study of the Yoruba language, published in the 1840s and 1850s. His role in producing the Yoruba bible, which set new standards for later African translations, was crucial.

Dear reader, don't you think there might just be someone

sitting in our pews today who can help in translating the bible into other local dialects in our country, thereby making it more accessible to several others. Don't you think there might just be someone sitting in our pews today who has been called to write literatures that will bring the message of the kingdom to our inner cities? Unfortunately, these people may never realize and harness their calling especially if the leaders of their churches do not encourage them in this direction. Hence, they may remain church-goers all their lives. How sad!

HIS MISSIONARY WORK

In the upper and middle Niger territories Crowther pioneered an early form of Christian-Muslim dialogue for Africa. He oversaw J.C. Taylor's ground-breaking work in Igboland and directed the evangelisation of the Niger Delta, with notable results at such centers as Bonny.

In the 1880s clouds gathered over the Niger Mission. Crowther was old, Venn dead. The morality of members of Crowther's staff was increasingly questioned by British missionaries. Mission policy, racial attitudes, and evangelical spirituality had taken new directions, and new sources of European missionaries were now available. Crowther's mission was dismantled: by financial controls, by young Europeans taking over, by dismissing, suspending, or transferring the African staff. Crowther, desolated, died of a stroke. An European bishop succeeded him.

Part of the Niger Mission retained its autonomy as the Niger Delta Pastorate Church under Crowther's son, Archdeacon D.C. Crowther, and at least one of the European missionaries, H.H. Dobinson, repented of earlier hasty judgments. Everyone recognized Crowther's personal stature and godliness; his place in the history of translation and evangelisation has often been undervalued.

FROM SLAVE TO MISSIONARY!

If one man who was taken away from the shores of the country into slavery, got saved and later went back to become a missionary in the same country from where he was taken captive, think of what will happen to our country if every person that gets saved in our churches went back into the world from where they were saved to become missionaries there. Do you even have an idea of what will happen to Nigeria in just a few short years?

This goes to show you how relevant the church is in the transformation of our country if we woke up. This also shows you how much we are depriving the nation of by our insensitivity and selfishness demonstrated in the way we do church today.

2.   Garrick Sokari Braide (1880 to 1918):

Garrick Braide is one of the pioneers of revival in Africa. Braide was born in 1882 in Obonoma, a small Kalabari pagan village in the Niger Delta (now Bayelsa, Delta and Rivers State in the South of Nigeria). This village was noted as one of the leading places of pagan worship and pilgrimage in Nigeria. His parents were servants of the Ogu cult which was a titular deity of Obonoma.

His parents were very poor; therefore Braide did not have the opportunity of being educated. He later became a Christian and was baptized on January 23rd 1910 at St Andrews Anglican Church in Bakana.

Garrick Braide was an Ijaw man by tribe, but he had to learn the Church catechism in Igbo language, as this was the language of instruction in all the Niger-Delta Pastorate. Braide had to learn the Ten Commandments, The Lord's Prayer and the Creeds in Igbo before he was baptised. After his baptism, he was confirmed by Rev. James Johnson.

Around 1912 Braide was beginning to be noted for his enthusiasm and religious exercises. He later felt called by the Lord into ministry and was accepted as a lay preacher in the Anglican Church of the Niger-Delta pastorate.

HIS WORK

Braide was baptized at Bakana in the Niger Delta Pastorate founded by Samuel A. Crowther. Later in 1915, he led a revival that featured mass baptisms, healing, Sunday observance, and active opposition to traditional religion and to imported articles, especially trade gin. Traditionalist complaints and accusations of being seditious led to Braide being imprisoned twice.

Wait a minute friend: how many of our churches and church leaders are being persecuted and imprisoned for standing for the Lord today? How many times do we hear of ministers and pastors upholding the truth of the kingdom to the point of being imprisoned? When we look at the ministry of Jesus and even the disciples after Him, we discover that they all faced severe persecution from the government and authority of the day because they were constantly speaking against the evils of the day. But today, what we have are churches that are full of the same set of people (politicians and non-politicians alike) who destroy the nation without the church ever batting an eyelid!

One of such stories that made the news in the national dailies was that of a man who was a banker. On a sunny afternoon, he walked into his pastor's office and paid a tithe of 10 million naira and the pastor blessed him. The Pastor turned a blind eye to the fact that the man's annual salary wasn't even up to 10 million let alone a hundred million naira. As far as the money was coming to the church, it was all fine. The bank in question would have become crippled if not that security operatives caught up with the perpetrator of the evil deed in time. Well, these sort of things happening in our churches have got to change. We must rise up against all ills in our society. The church is not a social gathering and must not be allowed to become one. For crying out loud, it is the ground and pillar of truth.

As for Braide, the initial Anglican welcome he received soon changed to opposition. Some members exited the Anglican Church for the movement Braide pioneered. This made the Anglican church initiate some indigenization reforms. A variety of "Christ's Army" independent churches honouring Braide also arose from the movement and they continued in south-east Nigeria.

BRAIDE'S NATIONAL IMPACT

Braide had a gift for healing. Beginning in 1908, people came to him for cures to illnesses and also prophecies. He was said to be able to predict personal difficulties and to bestow good fortune. Visitations to witch doctors also dramatically decreased as the people relied on God for healing.

Another influence Braide's preaching had on the Ijaw people was to convict them to set on fire their fetishes and charms. Braide moved from one village to another preaching the Gospel and telling the people to renounce their fetishes. Like the Biblical Gideon he stopped people from offering sacrifices to the great divinity of Kalabari. He had tremendous success in getting converts to cast out their fetishes and idols. He also challenged traditional priests in a rainmaking contest and then outshone them by invoking the Christian God.

Now, how much success can we say that our churches have had in terms of true conversion today? How many lives have been truly transformed through the ministry and effectiveness of our churches? By the way, when I talk about transformation, I am not talking about how many people we have succeeded in getting to sit and listen to us on Sundays. As we all know, that is the new normal in our churches today!

Do you know that some of the ladies who prostitute and hawk their bodies on various streets at night are registered members in some churches? Do you also know that some of the armed robbers on our streets and highways are confirmed members of different churches? Even those who steal with their pens in offices and government parastatals are workers and sometimes leaders in our churches! Needless to say is how the messages and coercion to give have made thieves out of our people today.

That is why I ask "how many of those we have succeeded in getting to sit and listen to us every day have been transformed? How many of them can God be proud of between Monday and Saturday? How many of them are making an impact in their world like they should? How many of them have we as a church given wings to fly?

Braide spent night vigils in prayer, enforced Sunday observance, and preached peace and reconciliation. He also denounced the use of alcohol so completely that consumption fell dramatically. As a result, the British administration faced a deficit of £576,000 in 1916, a loss which was ascribed to Garrick Braide's movement. The loss was so great that when the British moved against him in fear of his growing influence, they listed the decline in revenue as one of their charges!

Now, that is real tangible result right there in the area of national transformation. Fellow citizens of Nigeria, brothers and sisters, my heart goes out to the church in Nigeria today. It is so disheartening to see how depraved she has become. We have so deviated from the norm that evil has become the standard in our churches. Come to think of it, when was the last time you heard that a church was being sued for taking a stand against a government enrichment policy that was against the gospel of the kingdom? When was the last time you heard of a church and her leaders being persecuted for their involvement in national transformation?

Imagine Braide being charged for doing something that affected the government in such a significant way. That is what I call the kingdom influence friends. How much of that do we see today? All we have are churches that have become friends with the world and its system. But by God, all that must begin to change now. You and I must say no to the version of Christianity that condones evil, leaving us with only cancerous growths and development. We must say no to the kind of Christianity that is only in the favour of a few individuals rather than the general body of Christ.

By 1915, Braide had attracted a following more attached to him than to the Delta ministry or the CMS; his followers were estimated to number more than a million. He was honored as a prophet and began using that title, calling himself Elijah II. Braide had become the focus of a cult. Over two-thirds of the Delta congregation abandoned Bishop Johnson for Braide, and Johnson turned against his protégé.

After proscribing the movement for heresy, Johnson asked the British colonial authorities to investigate. They needed little prompting. When Braide was quoted as saying that power was passing from whites to blacks during World War I, the British imprisoned him for sedition.

CONFRONTING THE CHALLENGE OF THE DAY

Braide's method of teaching and ministry was very different from that of the Mission Churches. While they introduce Christianity through the teaching of the Creeds, The Lord's Prayer and catechism, Braide adopted a more practical approach and contextualized the Gospel among the Delta people. He taught the people to renounce their gods, destroy their fetishes and to simply believe in the Lord Jesus.

Braide was convinced that the approach of the Mission Churches did not deal with the root problems of the Delta people; namely idol worshipping. He knew that until the Delta people lost faith in their witch doctors, idols and fetishes there could be no true conversion. To this end he organized a crusade against charms, idol worshipping and the use of fetish objects.

Dear reader, look around you today and tell me ... what is the church of today doing about the challenges of the people today? How many churches are actually doing something tangible to affect their environment like we saw Braide doing? Instead what we have going on in our churches today is promotion of selfish interests.

We are busy building cathedrals and empires when the lives we should be focused on building aren't getting any better. In fact, in certain instances, it has been observed that people's growth and development rate drastically reduced when they associate with certain churches as compared to when they weren't members of any church.

Why is this so? Because our churches have become cold and dormant. Our churches have become heat coolants rather than heat generating centers. We now specialize in killing people's dreams and passion all in the name of religion. What a tragedy! The time for change has come. The time to take the church to a whole new level and realm of operation is here now. I challenge our clergy men and women, pastors, bishops, spiritual leaders in their entirety to discover the mind of the Father concerning the church and see to it that they build according to the pattern that God has shown to them.

THE CHURCH PEOPLE CAN RELATE WITH

Braide's methods of ministry redefined Christianity as a practical religion for the people of the Niger-Delta, and the result was a large number of conversions to the Anglican Church. Braide, using and encouraging the native language of the Ijaw people and not Igbo, made Christianity available to the average person. He reasoned from his own personal experience of learning the Church doctrines in Igbo that it took a long time, making it burdensome to become a Christian.

On the other hand, what we have today in Nigeria are churches that are fully westernized! We do everything western just to try to fit into a class we are not a part of. We sing, dress, preach and do everything else in line with what we have copied from the western world without realizing that they have different sets of challenges to deal with in their environment. In trying to meet up with these models, we have built cathedrals that the common man we are supposed to be reaching feels intimidated to be a part of! We dress and encourage a dress sense that keeps the underprivileged away from our churches.

In fact, I once heard of a situation where someone was refused from sitting in the front row in a certain church because he wasn't properly dressed! The ushers told him specifically that he knows the service is being videoed and he would most likely be picked by the camera if he sits in front. As such, he should sit somewhere at the back where he won't be featured on camera. The church was more concerned about their public image than anything else.

I remember when I just got born again too. I wanted to join a certain group in church then but I was bluntly refused. Why? Because I didn't have any shoes then! They said there was no way I would be allowed to be a part of that group without having shoes. The worst is that no one even though it wise to get one for me even when I made it clear I couldn't afford one! Tell me, is this the type of church that will affect the country? Is this the kind of church that will bring about the change we so earnestly desire? I am sorry but that can never happen unless things change.

That is why I am writing this book. I want to sensitize the Nigerian people to remember from where we have fallen and return to our first love. Let us learn from those who have gone ahead of us and recorded great success. Let's practice what they practiced and build on it to get even better results today. The church that will be relevant in nation building has got to be a church that is ministering to the locals. And there is no way we can minister to people if we will not be humble enough to come to their level.

MINISTRY EXPLOITS

Aided also by his ability to demonstrate the gift of healing through prayer, he was accepted by his people as a Prophet commissioned by God. The effect of Braide's preaching was evident in the number of those coming to the enquirers' class (a modern day equivalent of The Alpha Course).

His ministry spread from Bonny to Urhoboland, Benin and Yorubaland. Some Anglican ministers who supported Braide's ministry noticed that the statistical figures of those becoming Christians had risen steeply. The cross of Christ was erected in the place of idols, revival meetings were held with thousands of people attending and people were healed faster at Braide's meetings than in the care of the traditional or European doctors.

This goes without saying that enough of all these self-proclaimed deliverance ministers of today who are wasting time by conducting deliverance for their born-again church members whom Christ has already delivered. It is my prerogative that if anyone wants to really demonstrate God's power, then they should step out of the churches. I mean they should step out and go conduct these deliverance sessions in those places where idol worshipping is still very much being practiced.

Enough of all this deception that has kept God's people

bound for many years. Whereas we should be releasing God's people to go out and take over territories for God, we keep them coming back week after week casting the same set of demons out of them.

Dear brothers and sisters, even if the clergymen will not change, you must arise and change. You must begin to learn to study the bible for yourself and apply the truths therein to your life. Don't let someone keep you bound with deliverance upon deliverance when you should be out there making a difference in the world.

Our churches have been ineffective in national transformation because we have been busy with the wrong things. We have focused on the wrong matters when we should have been making progress. It was said that Garrick Braide achieved in three months what the Church Missionary Society (CMS) had not attained in half a century. I mean, he did more in three months than those who were playing church did in fifty years. I wonder what the comparison will be today if we had to compare what he did with what we are busy doing in our churches today!

Braide's ministry was a success in that there was an awakening in Nigeria which had never occurred before. Now is the time that churches must arise with a kind of awakening that we haven't seen before.

3.   Joseph Ayo Babalola (1904 - 1959):

Babalola was born of Yoruba parents at Ilofa, Nigeria, and was brought up as an Anglican. Having left elementary school, he was employed in the Public Works Department as a steam roller operator. In October 1928, while trying to repair his machine, he avowed that Jesus Christ called him to abandon the job and start preaching. He then joined Faith Tabernacle in Lagos, which was related to an American Pentecostal organization.

In September 1930 Babalola was credited with raising a dead man to life. From then on, with bell and Yoruba Bible in hand, he toured Yorubaland and eastern Nigeria, preaching about repentance, and renunciation of idolatry, the importance of prayer and fasting, and the power of God to heal sickness.

Dear readers, I understand that times have changed and development has come to the world. But should the need arise, how many of our pastors and preachers today will readily roll up their sleeves, go from village to village preaching the gospel? Or how many of them will even go from city to city preaching this gospel? Did our heroes of faith actually sit in one place building castles for themselves? The answer is no!

What we have today on-going in our churches are "executive pastors". These are more like CEOs of corporations whose ministries are confined to their air-conditioned offices and ultramodern church auditoriums! The problem with that is that a church that has no real contact with real people cannot change people's lives or change the country.

Joseph Babalola was known for preaching about repentance, and renunciation of idolatry and he had great success doing so. On the contrary, these sort of messages are very scarce on the lips of this present age church leaders.

A MAN OF PRAYER

Pa Apostle Joseph Ayo Babalola as he was fondly called once told his fellow ministers during a prayer meeting to kneel down for a SHORT prayer. After about 2-3 hours of kneeling down, the ministers became frustrated and sat down, leaving only Apostle Babalola still on his knees praying for about 5-6 hours. The following day, they asked him "Baba (Father), if you ask us to pray a short prayer with you which took almost 6 hours, how many hours will your LONG prayer then last for?"

One of the greatest tragedies that have befallen the church

today is the fact that it doesn't have the kind of quality leadership that the earlier men of faith had. I mean, when a pastor becomes a stranger in the presence of God, what do we expect from him? When a pastor becomes too busy devising means and ways to enrich himself and his organization, what do we expect from him?

No wonder some of the messages church members receive from churches today are far from being coined out of the word of God. Some pastors now preach their personal opinions as doctrines all in a bid to deceive the gullible! Ours has become a case of the blind leading the blind.

Apostle Joseph Babalola as well as other great ministers that have ever arisen in our country or anywhere in the world have always been men of prayer. They were people whose attention God had. They were people who listened to God and communicated His mind to the people. To this end, through this book, I am urging all clergymen and women in our country to follow after these worthy examples.

You may have heard of the Ori Oke Aanu (Mountain of Mercy) Praying Ground, Erio-Ekiti in Osun State Nigeria. The mountain of prayer was founded by this same Apostle Babalola. There is a spot on top of that mountain where he knelt to pray and his knee pierced through, leaving a giant hole in the rock due to his long hours in praying. That hole is still there till-date.

He was the only man that travelled overseas for missionary works without airplane or ship. Sometimes, when preaching the angel will lift-up his two legs and he will begin to move and float in the air without his feet touching the ground.

DEMONSTRATION OF REAL GOSPEL POWER

On the 9th of October 1928 at about 12 o'clock he was by his steamroller by the river Ariran, it was here he heard a loud voice from above like the roar of thunder which called his name thrice saying: "Joseph! Joseph!! Joseph. Leave this job you are doing; if not, this year you are going to be cut off from the earth."

Again on October 11, 1928, while trying to repair his machine, he heard an audible voice from the Lord to abandon the job and start preaching. That was how he received his calling and thereafter he began fasting and praying. The turning point in his early ministry came when he was commanded by God to go to his hometown to warn his people against idolatry, fetish practices and evil works.

"According to him; The Spirit told me to go to my hometown, where I was born. The Lord said I should rub my face with ashes and to carry palm leaves in my hand and to buy a bell, which I was to be ringing the moment I entered the town and I obeyed. The voice told me to tell my people that unless they repented, evil beasts would enter the town to destroy them.

On that same day I entered the town with a bell in my hand and there was a great stir and consternation as people fled when they saw me. The moment they set their eyes on me they fled. The voice told me to ring the bell in my hand round the town and I obeyed"

His people however refused to repent or change their ways they instead summarily beat him up and his family was subjected to heavy persecution by the people of the town. In defense against the prophesied invasion of the town by wild beasts the people of the town armed themselves with guns and cutlasses. However God told His servant to tell them he would not bring beasts again but instead would bring epidemics and it would start within forty- five days.

At the expiration of the prophesied forty-five days an epidemic of small pox broke out and within 3 weeks about 300 persons had died. But those who repented and those who came to the man of God after contracting the disease were spared. Ayo Babalola was sent out of the Anglican Church of his village by his Bishop because most members of the Church saw visions; spoke in tongues and prayed vigorously.

Oh, this makes me wonder what our country will be like if only our churches demonstrated such real gospel influence. Imagine that every church has such an influence on just one sector of our country. Think of what will happen if Church A demonstrates God's influence in economic matters and Church B does so in political matters while Church C does the same in our educational sector. Who will be left to say that "only God can save Nigeria"? For real, Nigeria would have gone past being saved and she would be the one saving other nations who haven't seen the light now, but it is better late than never. That is why I am bringing all these information across your way.

The power of God is not for making people fall down in church. The power of God is not for delivering those who have already been delivered. It is time we took that deliverance power to the sectors of our nation that need this deliverance desperately.

In 1930 Faith Tabernacle affiliated with the British Apostolic Church. Shortly after, following a schism in the Apostolic Church about 1940, Babalola went with a new independent church, Christ Apostolic Church (CAC), where he continued his healing and revivalistic activities until his death. The C.A.C regards Babalola as an apostle and his revival ministry as the beginning of the church. A CAC retreat center was built at Ikeji-Arakeji, Osun State where Babalola was first called in 1928.

The Christ Apostolic Church did not die along with Apostle Joseph Ayo Babalola in 1959. In fact it has grown rapidly over the years, with many churches under the Christ Apostolic Church name but each church with a specific branch name.

The Joseph Ayo Babalola University (JABU) a private Nigerian university located in Ikeji-Arakeji in Osun State, established by the Christ Apostolic Church (C.A.C) Worldwide is named after him, located at the same place where he was called by God in 1928.

4.   Mary Slessor (1848 - 1915)

Mary Slessor was a hard working Scottish mill girl and an unorthodox Sunday School teacher, who, inspired by David Livingstone, became a missionary in Calabar, Nigeria, an area where no European had set foot before – making her a ground breaking missionary.

Mary became a Christian at a young age. She enjoyed going to church; it was a wonderful outlet from her miserable home life. She was not well-educated, but loved to read, and would stay up late soaking up any book she could find. She loved reading the Bible most of all, studying Jesus and his life in the gospels. Mary dreamed of doing pioneer work in the remote interior of Africa.

At the time, missions work was mainly for men, so she was encouraged to get involved with home missions. It was her older brother who was planning to go as a missionary, but when Mary was 25 years old, he died. She wondered if maybe she could go in his place. Early in 1874 the news of the death of David Livingstone stirred the church and created a great wave of missionary excitement. Mary was then determined to go!

In 1875, Mary was accepted to go with the Calabar Mission. So, at age 27, she sailed for Calabar (located within present day Nigeria). She was stationed in Duke Town as a school teacher. Her living conditions seemed too nice for a missionary, and she was discouraged at how routine her job was. She learned Efik, the local language quickly and enjoyed teaching to some degree, but her heart was set on doing pioneer work. After three years, she was sent home on furlough because of malaria.

When she returned, she was given a new task in Old Town,

where she had the freedom to work by herself and live as she pleased. Mary decided to live with the local people as they lived. Her childhood of poverty made this lifestyle seem fairly normal. And, this way, she was able to save part of her missionary salary to send back to her family in Scotland.

TAKING GOD INTO THE SPHERES OF LIFE

Despite several bouts of illness and constant danger, she lived with the tribes, learned their language, and traditions, earning their respect and putting an end to some barbaric practices.

One custom that broke her heart was 'twin-murder'. The tribes thought that twins were a result of a curse caused by an evil spirit who fathered one of the children. Both babies were brutally murdered and the mother was shunned from society.

Overwhelmed and depressed, she knelt and prayed, "Lord, the task is impossible for me but not for thee, lead the way and I will follow." Rising, she said, "Why should I fear? I am on a Royal Mission. I am in the service of the King of kings. Thereafter Mary rescued many twins and ministered to their mothers. She was continuously fighting against this evil practice, often risking her life to stop the leaders from killing twins. The Lord gave her favour with the tribesmen, and Mary eventually gained a respect unheard of for a woman.

My question again to you dear readers is that, where are the Mary Slessors of our day? Where are the Mary Slessors in the various sectors and spheres of our society today? You see, it is not enough to pray and ask God to take control. It is not even pardonable to tell God that the task is impossible. What you ought to pray about is "Lord how can it be done!"

Just imagine that Marry Slessor did nothing about the killing of twins. Imagine that she was like we are today and paid deaf ears to the issues facing the people of her day. What do you think would have happened? In fact, I am sure that some of the so-called pastors who are tying people down in churches today may not have made it alive. Some of them or their parents might have been victims of that practice too!

It is high time our Christianity lost every sense of selfishness in it. After all, the Christian life that is revealed to us in scriptures is actually a selfless and self-giving one. That is why Jesus showed us the example by first laying down his life for us. If we are true followers of Christ, then we must be willing to go to any length to see that we affect others in a positive way too.

Our churches must stop this "I don't care attitude" that has eaten so deeply into our system. We must become a group of responsible people who are responsive to the challenge of the day both as individuals and as a body. Now is the time for our churches to identify the issues of the society that they must fix.

Just as Mary did something about the killing of twins, so also must we do something about female mutilation. So must someone from within our churches arise to do something about teenage marriage. Why can't our churches take the responsibility for education and other concerns of the society? Even if they can't cater to the educational need of the whole country, they can start from doing something about those within their community.

Only half the cost of some of our ultramodern auditoriums and cathedrals can go a long way to do something about the hungry children on the streets. Not just the streets of Nigeria as a whole but the same streets on which our churches are situated.

Pastors, ministers, clergy, I challenge you as a pastor myself. Let us rise to the occasion and shine the light in our nation again. I believe that the church has a super significant role to play in the transformation of our nation and I am calling on us all to take up the challenge that is before us. Let us begin to cast new visions for our churches and communities and see, if the resulting Nigeria will not be one we will all be proud of

DOMINATING ALL THE WAY

Mary was bold in her ministry and fearless as she travelled from village to village. She rescued hundreds of twin babies thrown out into the forest, prevented many wars, stopped the practice of trying to determine guilt by making people drink poison, healed the sick, and told the people about the great God of love whose Son came to the earth to die on the cross that sinful men might have eternal life.

Just for the records, this is one woman we are talking about here. One woman rescued hundreds of twins. The same woman prevented many wars, stopped the practice of determining guilt by making people drink poison and so on. This same person was also involved with healing the sick and eventually telling them about the great God and His love for them.

Now imagine for a moment that everyone who gathered in our churches did just one thing out of all these many things that Mary did. I mean, let's not even try to be Mary here. Let's just have one project handled by one member of church. If that happens, where do you think we will be as a nation in five years? Can you now see why the church is to blame for what has become of our country? Can you see why the church is in a perfect position to do something about our nation?

THE SHEPHERD WHO LAID DOWN
HER LIFE FOR THE SHEEP

Mary's lifestyle consisted of a mud hut (infested with roaches, rats, and ants), irregular daily schedule (normal in African culture), and simple cotton clothing (instead of the thick petticoats and dresses worn by most European women at the time). The other missionaries were unable to relate with her life. She epitomized the idea that the good shepherd lays down his life for the sheep unlike what is obtainable in our country today.

Sadly, it is the sheep that are laying down their lives for the shepherds. It is the sheep that goes hungry while the shepherds eat fat and large. The sheep get milked of their little income for the shepherds to ride on horses. How pathetic! We have turned the church into a religious slave trade system and this has got to change.

If a European woman can live in such a way that even other European missionaries were unable to relate to her lifestyle, what stops us from going down that route. Why invest so much in the material things of this world at the expense of real needs of real people. Why spend money in such a profligate manner and turn around to ask church people to pray and believe God for a miracle when they themselves are in need?

This attitude will definitely cripple the church and make her irrelevant in nation building. A church that will be relevant in this day and time has got to understand that it must invest into people rather than buildings and structures.

In 1915, nearly 40 years after coming to Africa, Mary Slessor died at the age of 66 in her mud hut. Many years after her death, she is still an inspiration to all who hear her story. She was not only a pioneer missionary, but also a pioneer for women in missions and an example for the church today.

5.   Archbishop Benson Idahosa (1938-1998)

He was a man that has been adjudged by Christian folks as the father of Pentecostalism in Nigeria. He was the founding president of the Pentecostal Fellowship of Nigeria (PFN). He is regarded as the bulldozer that cleared the way for many of the ministries that came afterwards! In fact, many prominent Nigerian pastors like Ayo Oritsejafor, David Oyedepo, Felix Omobude, Fred Addo, Bishop Mike Okonkwo and Chris Oyakhilome were his protégés. So we can safely say that his influence cuts across several ministries in and outside the country today.

He began the television ministry in Nigeria in those days. He was the first to make it possible for the gospel to be preached on TV. He used to go to the television station to preach live on the set. Then people criticized him for using the television. Some began to call the television "devil's box". But Idahosa didn't allow that bother him.

Idahosa also brought drum sets and guitars into the church and they called him a disco church. There is no minister in Nigeria to compare to him when he was alive. He was a pioneer who cleared the way. And all of those who condemned him and criticized him have now eaten their own words.

THE CHURCH AND THE GOVERNMENT OF THE LAND

Archbishop Benson Idahosa related with the government of the day the way the prophets of old would do. He was always on a corrective mission to government officials and heads of state. When Abacha took over, he took some other bishops with him to see Abacha at Aso Rock. While at the state house he said:

"Abacha I did not come to pay homage, I have come to advise you. You cannot stay here without my prayer."

His role with the government was essentially to tell them what to do and what they have not done right. Abacha allowed him to pray for him. Bishop Ilemobo was with him that day too. Idahosa related with the Abacha government in the capacity of an advisor and he was not bought over. He warned Abacaha not to treat Nigerians with impunity. He also warned him not to toy with Nigerians. That was what he went there to do. But a lot of people thought he was there to pay homage and show support for Abacha.

Oh how I wish that the church will understand her position

in nation building and reclaim it. How I wish that the church today will get back to that original position of being a guide to the government rather than being an instrument in the hands of the government.

Idahosa did not tell Abacha to leave the place for Abiola because he didn't want to be involved in the politics. He told Abacha to realize that people were suffering and that he should think of the welfare of the masses. Frankly, Nigeria is more than anyone's personal ambition. Making a case for Abiola would have been political and he did not want to be involved in the power game of politics.

For the records, Idahosa was Abiola's very good friend. There was a time his Concord Press did a report that was not complimentary on Idahosa, he stormed the press and went to them saying these words, "Concord you are dead, I close you down you won't function again for this wrong reporting. After that Abiola started looking for Idahosa everywhere probably to set the records straight with him.

How many of our churches today have the boldness to confront the evils in our day and speak the truth? How many will still uphold the truth of the word of God in the face of natural relationships with the men and leaders of the land? Little wonder why our churches have become so powerless in the land. Many have become puppets in the hands of power hungry men who have no good intentions whatsoever for the land. It is high time the church became known for standing for the truth rather than taking sides. It is time that our men of God stood up and spoke the mind of God concerning our land even in the face of persecution and threats to their lives.

THE SPREAD OF IDAHOSA'S MINISTRY

A piece on the website of the USA branch of Idahosa's church had these to say:

- He pioneered the establishment of over 5,000 churches in Nigeria and parts of Africa;
- He took the gospel to 143 nations;
- He pastored the fifth largest church in the world in his time;
- He hosted his daily and weekly "Idahosa and You" television and radio programmes for 20 years; through the programmes he reached millions of people in Africa and impacted lives in the Muslim territories,
- He garnered four degrees, including two doctorates from four different institutions;
- He authored many books and produced thousands of audio tapes and videos of his messages.

To continue the work that he started, the Benson Idahosa University was named after him in 2002. During the Tomato fruit infection recently, the management of the university announced that the institution's faculty of agriculture would produce 800,000 tons of Tomatoes! That is what I call contribution to national development by the church!

If you are wondering what has become of the church he left behind, the answer, in the words of a 2006 report by Bishop Harry Westcott, an Australian pastor and associate of the late Idahosa is this: "the work, witness and outreach of CGM (Church Of God Mission Int'l) are in great shape and obviously growing at a consistent rate. When Archbishop Benson died in March 1998 CGM had one hospital, it now has four! It had one bible school, it now has six! It had 98 primary and secondary schools, it now has 104...

Imagine what our country Nigeria will be like if every church had just one hospital or built and sponsored the running of just one primary or secondary school. What will become of Nigeria if every church extended a hand of help to the society to solve at least one of its various problem? This is exactly what must become of our nation in this day and time. Churches must understand their role in nation building and go beyond just keeping people in pews.

TYING IT UP TOGETHER

While it is laudable that these heroes of faith have made an impact in Nigeria in terms of delivering us from the shackles of idolatry, the fact remains that there is still much to be done. There is much more to be accomplished.

While Moses delivered the Israelites out of bondage and into the Promised Land, over in the Promised Land, it was a different ball game. In the Promised Land, there was a new need. This time, it wasn't a need for deliverance but a need to build. It was time to begin to work, farm and all that.

The church today must recognize that there is a whole new challenge on the horizon. Her responsibility today has gone beyond just deliverance from idolatry. It is high time the church began to encourage and motivate its members to go out there and tackle the problems facing the country. It is high time the churches began to show their members how they can carry the kingdom influence to their respective areas of operation and concern through skillful application of the principles I am showing you in this book.

It is not enough for the churches as organizations to do something. Every individual in church has got to find his own place and demonstrate dominion there by being the light. Every member has got to be trained to be the saviour in the various sectors and areas of human endeavours in our country.

I will be elaborating more on the practical steps you can take to begin making a difference big time in the next part of this book. So for now, let's move on to seeing some details of how the church has misled her people over the years and what should be done instead.

CHAPTER 7

Doctrines of the Nigerian Church That Inhibit Growth & Development

Doctrines of the Nigerian Church That Inhibit Growth & Development

Having looked at what the heroes of faith accomplished, I am sure you can begin to see the places where we have missed it today and probably things we can do to move things forward. Now, I want to take some time to shed some more light on a few of the doctrines that are being perpetuated in our country today that has added to the abysmal condition in which our country has found herself in.

Doctrines of Fear: Oh how saddening it is to know that our preachers have become fantastically good at preaching fear. They preach how that we should fear the devil. How that we should fear demons and fear the powers of darkness, the occultic, witches, witchcraft, voodoo, black magic etc. There is even a popular saying amongst the tribe from which I hail from – the Yorubas. They often say that the devil has got tremendous power but that what he lacks however is salvation - indeed! That is arrant nonsense my friends.

From whence did he get the power? The same devil that Jesus spoke about that he saw falling like a lightening from heaven. Is it the same devil that the bible describes that Jesus spoiled and disarmed and made a public display of? Is it the same devil that Jesus says He has given us the authority to trample upon and upon all his abilities? Come on friends, stop making a ridicule of our heavenly Father.

But not to leave the subject at hand, this is the same message that is being preached back at home in my country – Nigeria. Pastors even preach that God sends sickness to humble a man and discipline him. Oh I hear of all sorts of prayer being prayed back at home. Prayers that border on God destroying your enemies. Enemies in mother's house and father's house. I hear of prayers that are centered on breaking free from the hold of ancestral and generational curses. But more disturbing is the fact that these prayers are being prayed day in day out in the churches.

The same prayers that are prayed on Sundays are the same ones that will be prayed on Friday night during vigil and it is the same ones that will keep being repeated from the first day you set foot into the church and for as long as the members remain there. This is so unfortunate.

Little wonder why the believers have been so ineffective in causing a revolution in our dear nation. How can a people who are so busy touting and promoting the devil and his abilities ever get to make a difference in the society. There just isn't anyway to make that happen.

Doctrine of Selfishness and Paganism: Another doctrine that is being circulated is that of selfishness and paganism. Church members go to churches these days only to hear of how God will bless them and prosper them. They are being told of how God will help them to win the contract they are pursuing and get them the visa they are after even ludicrous things such as God helping them to win a lottery.

Sometime ago, I heard of a particular congregation where some of the church members were playing lottery. When it was time for them to select their lucky numbers, they called the pastor on phone and gave him 3 numbers on which he was supposed to pray. And thereafter, he was supposed to come up with answers from the spirit telling them which of the numbers was the winning one.

Did he pray? Oh sure he did and promptly presented a number to them. Did they win the lottery? Your guess is as good as mine. Heavens no! But this is the kind of doctrine that is being propagated in our churches. A doctrine of praying for earthly mundane things; the likes of cars, employment opportunity, houses, money etc. That is, a doctrine that takes man's attention away from God and places the focus on self.

Is it wrong to want a car or a house? No? Definitely not? But should it be your focus? No as well! A capital no. And the reason is clear in scriptures, when you seek God and His righteousness, all of the above and more will be added to you. Again, with all of these petty and mundane things occupying our attention, no wonder believers have been ineffective. No wonder they have not been able to step up in their roles as national sons that ought to bring about transformation in the nation.

Doctrines That Enslave, Imprison, Cripple and Paralyze God's Children: This is another kind of message that has gained popularity in our churches back home in Nigeria. A message that is centered around God's children obtaining deliverance from all manner of things ranging from generational curses to ancestral curses, to mammy water spirts and all of such. And this is what those believers hear day in, day out being preached in the services.

As a matter of fact, there are special services for conducting these deliverances and this has reduced God's children to beggars. Slaves and beggars who are always in need of one form of deliverance or healing. As such, services woven around these themes (healing and deliverance) are the order of the day in many churches but this ought not to be so.

The bible shows us that healing is the children's bread and they ought not to beg or plead or even pay for it as is the custom in some churches. But they ought to claim it and appropriate it in their own lives. However the reverse is taught in our churches. These kinds of messages are paralyzing and debilitating to the human soul.

And guess what? Those who are subjected to these messages can't even dare think of taking responsibility for a nation when they haven't taken responsibility for their own lives. No wonder Nigeria is in the calamitous state that she is in today.

Speaking about a gospel that enslaves and paralyses, there is a church I heard about where the Pastor told the members to come to church with some water that he was going to pray on for them. Now, some people went to the service with the popular sachet water in Nigeria which is about a liter of water in size. But the majority went to the church with as much as 5litres of water and some even 10 liters. Do you know what happened thereafter?

After the Pastor prayed on the water, he gave an instruction that nobody should leave the church until they have finished every last drop of water they brought. That was where the battle began. People started struggling to finish up their large volumes of water because they dared not disobey the Pastor. This is really pathetic.

Whereas children of God ought to be trained, equipped, developed and raised up as sons. Sons who are responsible for themselves and their society at large, they are being treated as slaves and ordinary servants.

I even hear of churches where the church members pay money at the gate in order to attend services. How can this be? And some other Pastors request their members to pay money when they request that the pastors pray for them concerning a particular situation they are going through. If all these stories are really true, little wonder why Nigeria, a nation with about 50% of its citizens being Christians is a colossal failure today.

Doctrines of Trade by Barter: This is another doctrine that has been popularized in our churches in Nigeria. Preachers have made it such that except you bring an offering or a sacrifice, God will not hear you or have anything to do with you. Hence Pastors come up with all manner of offerings for church members to give. These offerings range from first-fruits to seed faith, prophet offering, thanksgiving seed and many other special offerings. These are all in a bid to make merchandise and profits off of God's children. It is such a shame.

Doctrines of Self-Righteousness: As good as this kind of doctrine sounds yet it is one of those doctrines that enslave and limit a man. The reason is this. When a person has given his heart to Christ and gotten saved, the next thing is to train the person to become both mature in the things of God and in the affairs of this world. In other words such a person ought to be taught the principles and values of the kingdom of God. He should be taught to imbibe God and carry His nature. He should be raised in such a way that the Word becomes flesh in him. And on the flip side, the believer should also be trained to become a kingdom carrier and a kingdom imposer in the sphere of life that he is concerned with.

For him to be able to do this, he's got to be trained to be an expert in that field. He has to become an authority so that people can listen to him. For starters he even needs to know the sphere of life where he wants to impose the kingdom on. When he has identified it, he should then go ahead and get the required knowledge to become the very best in that field. Knowledge that will make him become a professional, a specialist, by every definition, a master in that field.

And where else is better to encourage people to become the very best in their fields, callings and in their gifts, church.

But rather, what do we have in our churches?

Preaching on holiness, sin consciousness, preaching on how not to make mistakes so that the people can make heaven. However, the more Pastors talk about these things the more believers fall into errors and make mistakes. Because of a very simple principle i.e. a man is a product of the sum total of the words he is exposed to day in, day out.

Think about it yourself. You will agree with me that some of the mistakes you have made in life are the very same things that were constantly being drummed into your ears that you shouldn't do. Either by your parents, at church, your teachers or even things you read up yourself. Why is this so? Why did you fall into those same errors? The same principle i.e. you are a product of the words that you receive day in, day out. As you kept hearing those words, they occupied your mind. Subconsciously, you attracted the necessary scenarios to make those mistakes to yourself.

All of these messages being preached is what has kept the children of God subjected, defeated and in bondage. They have become prisoners of the doctrines and philosophies of life they have been exposed to. And they have become victims of a nation that keeps degenerating day after day.

WHAT NEEDS TO CHANGE?

This in my opinion is a very simple matter. One of the things that need to change is that Pastors should give up their roles as prison warders and instead become raisers of sons. What do prison warders do? They supervise inmates in prison and exercise control over them amongst other things. Isn't it the same thing that many Pastors in Nigeria are doing? Aren't they also maintaining a tight leash on their members' neck keeping them as ordinary church members instead of raising them to be kingdom carriers? Aren't they exercising control over them so that they don't become influential and independent and come to strive for their pulpit with them?

Isn't it true that these members are not trained to become giants in the different spheres of the country of Nigeria? Isn't it also true that the majority of those who attend churches in Nigeria are only trained to be in one departmental group or the other? As a matter of fact, chances are that even you reading this book is either a member of the choir, ushering department, decoration team, welfare, technical team or an instrumentalist. The rest are the administrative team, prayer band, evangelism, outreach team, Sunday school teachers, bible study teachers or pastoral care. The list is inexhaustible.

Another thing that we need to do in order to bring about a

change in our nation is to expunge all of the man-made doctrines and philosophies of life from our pulpit. And then the message of the Kingdom returns to it. Messages that border on sons arising in the church and taking responsibility for the affairs of the country. Messages that border on God's children identifying their own areas of passion or burden and go impose the Kingdom of God there. Messages that stir up the heart of believers to go and impose the kingdom of God on any area of the country they so choose or desire. These are the kinds of messages that need to be returned to our pulpits. Messages that are inspiring, uplifting, empowering. Messages that challenge God's people to bring light to every area of darkness in the country.

I still remember vividly the events that happened to me when I started writing articles about politics in Nigeria during the last presidential election. Oh too many people wrote to me saying I shouldn't get involved with politics. They told me politics is too dirty. Many others said point blankly that as a Pastor I should face my calling. Others even said that I have lost my vision, calling and anointing. People were writing all sorts of things including Pastors.

Note-worthy however is that some of these people spoke out of genuine concern for me. They tried to make me understand that politics is full of darkness and occultism. And as a result, for my own good, I should rather stay out of it, they warned. But wait a minute, if politics is full of darkness, is that not the more reason for me to be involved with it? I think that the fact that it is full of men of darkness and occultic affiliations is the more reason why I should be involved. If it is as dark and dirty as they say it is, then the more reason why the sons of God should arise and shine the light of God there.

The darker the sphere of life is, the more sons should arise and get involved with it. And this really makes sense when you think of the fact that we have been made the light of the world. As the light of the world, we've got a responsibility to shine.

And our shining is not within the four walls of the church. Our shining as believers is not useful amongst other believers in the church. Instead our shining should be carried out to those spheres of life, sectors and areas that are enshrouded in darkness. In the midst of darkness is where the beauty of light will be appreciated

Unfortunately, almost every sector of our nation is currently cloaked in darkness. The political sector, educational, entertainment, industrial, media, banking and finance, economic, medical, judiciary, housing and every sector that makes a society thrive.

Yet God's children are busy singing "Oh Lord, come down and manifest your power" Really? For how long? For how long will we sing the songs of bondage? For how long will we murder our peace and sanity? For how long will we lay a foundation of agony for our children and generations yet unborn? For how long are we going to wield the guillotine around our own necks and be the murderers of our own dreams? Oh I ask, for how long are we going to be our own slave masters oppressing and repressing our chances at happiness?

For goodness sake, He has already come! He has already manifested His power. As a matter of fact, if there is any manifestation left to be done, we are the ones to do so. We are the ones that the whole world is waiting and groaning for our manifestation right now. All God is doing is waiting on us to take up the responsibility that has been committed to us.

THE WHOLE EARTH IS WAITING FOR THE MANIFESTATION OF THE SONS OF GOD.

The whole earth is waiting for sons who will arise and emerge and take healing, deliverance, restoration, salvation and help to the ailing sectors of our nations. The attention right now in our country should be on sons who will arise. That is why I wrote this book too. This is part of my strategy to contribute my quota into the development and advancement of our dear nation.

I happened to be a part of the Clinton Foundation and was invited to a meeting of the board members of the foundation. The people in that meeting included: Bill Gates, Warren Buffet, Sir Richard Branson, myself as well as some other people. Guess what the discussion was all about? We were all taking up one global problem or the other that we were going to eliminate!

This is exactly how sons of God should think. One person should arise and put a stop to the Boko Haram menace. One person should put a stop to child marriages that lead to all manner of complications. Some other persons should arise and put a stop to corruption, power failure issues, bad infrastructures, bad roads, poor healthcare, high unemployment rate, insecurity of lives and properties, bad governance, eradication of laws that subjugate fundamental human rights, low standards of education, hunger, poverty, pollution, high rate of infant mortality etc.

I remember that when I started writing about politics in my country, people started saying a lot of things telling me that politics is dirty, it is darkness, you cannot dabble into it without being involved in the occultic.

However, it is sad that many have misunderstood my intentions. Many have had the wrong interpretation of my motives, but that is not to say that I am bothered about it. In fact, that is the part of the Nigerian mindset that has got to change. To set the records straight though, going into politics does not even qualify for the last thing on my mind. It's not even an agenda I have at all. However, one thing I do know is that I have to contribute my own quota to the development of our nation just as I have done even in a foreign land.

This was exactly how we developed the nation of Ukraine through the church I'm pastoring here in Ukraine. We made an extensive list of all the problems of the nation and then I started training people, challenging them to find their own sphere of calling, passion or the areas they want to go and influence and dominate.

The people I trained were nobodies. Ordinary people. Just like David who only had the distressed, debtors and discontented of life with him at one phase of his life but after spending an extensive time with him, listening to his teachings they later became mighty men who were reputed for their acts in the scripture. They were subduing Israel's enemies. But the point is that they did something for which they were later referred to as mighty men.

If we are taught that we should only pray for things to change then that's how we will live but if we are taught that we have the capacity to change things, then this will influence our lives.

So dear friends, awake from your slumber and get busy. It is time to carry the kingdom with you to your sphere of influence and operation. It is time to do away with the "only God can save Nigeria" mentality and adopt the "God has me here to change things" mentality!

IT'S TIME TO MEET GOD'S NEEDS TOO

You see, God is desperately in need. But His needs are not material or some petty mundane things. He is not in need of the same kind of things we crave for. Rather He is seriously in need of sons, deliverers, mighty men and saviors who will take responsibility for the affairs of the nation of Nigeria. He is in need of individuals that will arise to face the challenges of the day and bring about the much needed change in our society beginning with their own area of influence and concern.

Most especially, God is looking for His children to arise and take up the responsibility for national development. He is tired of Christians praying and chorusing everywhere "only

God can save Nigeria", when non-Christians are taking advantage of their human potentials to do great things.

I'm concerned about the children of God who ought to know better and who ought to be taking up the responsibility of fixing our nation but are not doing so. And this is a shame to the Body of Christ in general because at least believers go to church, they pray to God, they read the bible. Yet, they have left the affairs of the world in the hands of the sons of men!

The fact is that we are better positioned to change this world but ironically we are the ones who have done worse in exploring the earth than the sons of men who are not even believers.

It is clear looking at statistics of inventions, discoveries and fortune 500 companies, that it is not the believers that are managing the affairs of the earth. What a tragedy!!! As a matter of fact, let us explore some famous self-professed atheists and agnostics who have changed the world.

FAMOUS ATHEISTS AND AGNOSTICS WHO HAVE CHANGED THE WORLD

It is so ironic that the most celebrated developments and inventions of the world we live in today were not invented by religious people. In fact, in most of the cases, they weren't by people who knew or believed in God at all!

Think about the famous Thomas Edison. Did you think he was such a religious person? Do you think he was able to accomplish all he did because he prayed tirelessly? No my friend, that was not the case with him. Actually, one of his quotations actually reads:

"I have never seen the slightest scientific proof of the religious ideas of heaven and hell, of future

life for individuals, or of a personal God. He also did say that: So far as religion of the day is concerned, it is a damned fake... Religion is all bunk."

That was from a man who went on to make a significant impact in the world! But that is not all. Here is yet another statement by him:

"I cannot believe in the immortality of the soul... I am an aggregate of cells, as, for instance, New York City is an aggregate of individuals. Will New York City go to heaven? No; nature made us -- nature did it all -- not the gods of the religions."

What about the likes of Bill Gates, Mark Zuckerberg, Steve Jobs and so on? Were these men really the most religious of men? Were they the ones that went to church the most? Were they the ones that prayed the most? Or did you ever read that any of them was a choir master or cell group leader in their churches? Emphatically no!

These were all simple men who realized the enormous potentials available in the human person and decided to explore it to the fullest. They are ordinary men who dared to take advantage of all that God has placed in us humans and change the world of their day. So if without knowing God, they accomplished all these, shouldn't we who know and worship God be able to do much more? Shouldn't we be better positioned to change the world and change our country? But no, we will rather sit with folded arms chanting our national chorus "only God can save Nigeria".

STUNNING REVELATION OF THE TOP 10 COMPANIES IN THE FORTUNE 500 LIST

Before I go on to share the shocking revelation of the list of the top ten companies in the fortune 500 list, I will like to actually show you the list. Here you go:

1. Walmart

2. Exxon Mobil

3. Apple

4. Berkshire Hathaway

5. McKesson

6. UnitedHealth Group

7. CVS Health

8. General Motors

9. Ford Motors

10. AT&T

How many of these did you notice belongs to church or religious people? How many of them are being run by people who pray a lot or attend services the most? Where are the prayer warriors of our time? Where are the church faithful ones of our time?

Why is it that they are not the ones topping the chart? Is it because believers are a nation of mediocres? No, I personally don't believe so. But I do know that every man produces only to the capacity of their philosophies of life or doctrines as we Christians call it. Every man is a product of the words that he is being fed with on daily basis.

Our churches and their members haven't been able to match up to the rest of the world because of what I call the deception of religion! Rather than we sitting down and getting involved with activities that actually result in development and growth, we would rather be locked up in churches morning, noon and night praying and asking God to take control of our country.

In the midst of all that, the rest of the world is moving forward and making progress!

I blame this on the kind of message and doctrines we are constantly being fed with in our churches. I blame this on the messages that the majority of the church have been exposed to. But I believe that the time for change has come. The time for total transformation is here and we will make it happen together.

By the way, in the coming chapters, I will be showing you how to practically begin to take over territories for the kingdom. I will show you how that beginning right from where you are right now, you can make a difference that will outlive you like the heroes of faith did. Never again will you join them to chant the chorus that "only God can save Nigeria".

CHAPTER 8

A Necessary
Paradigm Shift

A Necessary Paradigm Shift

If you have been following the conversation thus far, it is likely that you may be thinking that I am out to castigate the heroic men and women of God who have served God faithfully in our churches. But in all honesty, that is far from being true. I mean, I am a pastor myself so the last thing I want to do here is to make a mockery of pastors.

However, I must not fail to state that while the great men and women of God that have served in the churches have done a great job at bringing the church to where it is today, there is still more to be done. The church as it is today is still very far away from what the Lord told us He is coming for. It is still far from a church without spots, wrinkles or any such thing.

Yes the church in Nigeria isn't exactly where it used to be in the early days when the missionaries brought the gospel to us but if the truth must be told, it is still a far cry from what it can be. Our generation of believers have the responsibility to take the gospel even further. We have the responsibility to conquer some more territories and to expand the influence of the kingdom to a higher horizon. That is why I talk about a necessary paradigm shift.

MOSES VS JOSHUA MODEL

One of the things I love about the word of God is that it gives us real answers to real questions. No matter what the area of concern might be, you will always find some wisdom to help when you look in there. The only problem I have observed is that most people are too lazy to study. And sadly, the same applies to even those who are preachers themselves.

That explains the reasons why most Christians know little or nothing about what God really says about certain important matters.

I remember the story of Moses and Joshua. Particularly, I am considering the difference in their respective leadership models. Something I want you to understand upfront is the fact that these two men led the exact same people. The major difference is that while Moses dealt with the fathers and older generation, Joshua dealt with their children.

So we find that in dealing with both generations, God adopted two distinctly different patterns and that is what I want to show you here. In Moses, case, God needed him to liberate His people from Egypt to their land of promise. In doing so, God wrought several mighty works of miracle all the way. Beginning from when they were in Egypt leading up to their sojourn in the wilderness, God was performing miracle after miracle.

I would bet that if you had met an Israelite then and asked him how they were going to fix any problem that faced them, he would gladly tell you that God will take care of it. And as for that time, that would have been right. When they got hungry, God went to the extent of sending them manna from heaven. God took it upon Himself to supply them with freshly baked manna every single day.

Like a comedian once said, God probably opened up a special wing of the kitchen in heaven to meet their daily needs. God was so committed to providing them with this manna that He even told them not to bother saving any for the following day. I mean they were so guaranteed of fresh manna every single day. Talk about complacency! Imagine a world where no one ever thought of getting into the kitchen because God was taking care of their stomach infrastructure all the way from heaven.

When they got thirsty, God didn't relent either. Even though they were right in the middle of a desert with no natural known means of getting water, God brought in the supernatural again. He made rocks produce water for them to drink. This was pampering at its peak if you ask me.

When they even got tired of manna and cried out to God for meat, He still answered them! The bible says that He caused a wind to blow quails into their camp. He supplied them in more quantities than they could possibly have just to show them that He is God and nothing is impossible or difficult for Him to do.

Somehow, it appears to me that the majority of the Nigerian believers today are only familiar with that regime or dispensation. They are only familiar with the God that led the Israelites out of Egypt into the land of Canaan. That explains why they keep clamouring that "only God can save Nigeria". They seem to be familiar with the God who will go out of His way and do anything to cater for the needs of His children as they journeyed to their land of promise. So they expect Him to make one supernatural move and let everything that is wrong with Nigeria be fixed. What they do not understand is that there has long been a paradigm shift. There has long been a change of model and modus operandi.

Dear friends, it is time to start down playing on miracles in our churches. It is time we began to emphasize the importance and dignity of labour. Our churches must start training people in the areas of skill development. Our churches must get involved with raising a new breed of Nigerians. A breed that will take up the responsibility for agriculture, manufacturing and construction industries, power, educational institutions and every single problem that is facing our country today.

So instead of sticking to the old model, we must now begin to familiarize ourselves with the new model. We must all begin to learn how the new model functions and then position ourselves rightly. The bible records in Joshua 5:12 that:

> *"Then the manna ceased on the day after they had eaten the produce of the land; and the children of Israel no longer had manna, but they ate the food of the land of Canaan that year."* (Jos 5:12)

What! You mean the manna ceased? Wow! That must have been some form of bad news for those who might have become used to that system. Those who were born in the wilderness who never knew anything other than manna might now find it difficult to adjust. But God was not perturbed about that. The days of free manna were over and gone forever. It was now time for them to eat the fruit of the land. It was time to enjoy the milk and honey of the land God had brought them into.

Listen my dear, in the new order, God doesn't send manna from heaven. He doesn't open up rocks to provide the people with water neither does He send wild winds to blow meat into the camp of the people. They now have to get up and do some work. It was time for them to begin to do some farming I tell you.

It would now be completely out of place for anyone to wake up in the morning and run outside in hope that manna may have fallen overnight as usual. It would be wrong for anyone to say he is not going to till the ground but would just wait for God to provide.

The same analogy is so true with the body of Christ today. Our fathers of faith have done a great job delivering our nations from the clutches of idolatry and witchcraft through signs and wonders. Today however, a new generation must arise to take their works further. This generation must rely less on signs and wonders but rely more on developing skills and building industries. This generation must rely less on the "Sidon look" model and take a proactive move towards bringing forth their desired result in our nation.

It is now prohibited for anyone to say "only God can save Nigeria". It is now out of place to sit and do nothing while expecting a miracle. It is even out of place to just pray and pray without doing anything. The church must wake up from its slumber and begin to take over the various parastatals of human endeavour.

We must now take responsibility for the building and development of industries. We must go out there and get involved with the production of goods and services that will meet the needs of the common man. We must all find our passion and place of assignment and reign there.

THE ROLE OF THE CHURCH IN BUILDING NIGERIA

The doctrines that have been preached in our churches in Africa and globally have not been helpful in raising believers to dominate the earth. We have mainly been taught to just stay in the church, be faithful, serve the church, and serve the man of God period. We have been taught that all that matters is to make sure you make heaven, avoid sin, be holy and you won't go to hell. Mission accomplished!!! But is that really all there is to being a Christian? Is that really all there is for the church to accomplish?

It is time we understood that the church is here to train its people in the doctrine of the kingdom. The church is here to raise men and women who will reign and dominate in their spheres of influence. As such, its effectiveness is a measure of how many it trains in that light rather than how many it gathers. Our attention must move from gathering people to actually training them. We must begin to train and raise people to become mature and responsible sons of God.

To achieve this, the messages coming from our altars must change. We must have a shift! I call it a "CHURCHSHIFT" It is time for us to move on to our promised land!!! It's time to begin to believe that with God on our side we can build a prosperous nation and continent.

The gospel that has been preached in our churches has not been fair to the African continent. It has left us in a beggarly state, waiting on God for things we could produce by and for ourselves. Our churches are full of people during work hours, morning, noon, evening, praying instead of being in the factories, libraries, laboratories, facilitating economic growth. We need a shift in our message and in our pulpit.

We must now begin to show people that the development we all crave for is in their hands. God has deposited something ingenious in each and every one of us. He has put something in us for the benefit of our beloved country.

Just imagine that every Christian in Nigeria took a hold of this message and went out there to do something. Imagine that every one of us only dared to fulfill the first out of the 7-fold instruction God gave man in the book of Genesis where He said to be fruitful! What do you think will become of a country with 80 million fruitful people? What will become of a nation where 80 million people were productive? Can you see that the problem of Nigeria is largely one we have created for ourselves? Our idleness and lack of spiritual understanding is what has kept us where we are.

THERE IS NO EXCUSE FOR INDOLENCE

It is saddening to admit that our churches often-times contribute immensely to the failure of the church and its people to rise to the occasion in Nigeria. I remember hearing of a certain church where the people are actually taught that what mattered most in their lives was their religious devotion to God. They are taught that attending services regularly and praying were the most important things in life. In fact, they support their argument with a scripture that I will like to bring to your notice right away.

> *"Unless the LORD builds the house, they labor in vain who build it; unless the LORD guards the city, the watchman stays awake in vain.2 it is vain for you to rise up early, to sit up late, and to eat the bread of sorrows; for so He gives His beloved sleep."* (PSALM 127:1-2)

They say that according to this scripture, all efforts of man is useless. It is no use for us to labor and exert ourselves trying to build our country. Rather, our focus should be on trying to get God to build our country for us they say. So they teach that people should sit back and let God come and build the country for us. But the simple question I have for them is this: can you point out a country in the world that was built by God? Can you pick up the map and identify a country that is doing well because God is the one building it?

Isn't it high time we stopped turning the scriptures around? Isn't it time we stopped using the scriptures to propagate our selfish interests? This scripture does not in any way condemn the role and importance of work. It does not connote that we should just do nothing but pray and wait for God.

It simply advices against us denying the input of God in our affairs. We must all acknowledge that it is God who gives us the wisdom and the strength that we put to work to produce great things. It is the absolute exemption of God from our affairs that the scripture warns against and not our inactivity please.

Yes it is true and I believe that God needs to bless the works of our hands, but you still need to do some work for God to bless it. You need to step out to build before God could bless what you are building. You need to guard the city before God could protect it for you.

However, in our own case we no longer produce labourers, we would rather pray to God to send labourers to come and build our cities. We refuse to put guards on duty, we would rather pray for God's protection. What a doctrine!

My brothers and sisters prayers and faith in God do not negate professionalism and dignity of labor. It does not rule out the importance of using our hands. It is only the man that has done his best that qualifies to ask for God's protection and blessings. This message must return to our pulpit.

WAS IT GOD THAT BUILT THE CITY OF DUBAI?

Have you ever heard the story of the city of Dubai before? Can you prove that it was God who came to help them turn a city that was once best described as a desert into one of the most advanced economies in the world? Was it God that came to turn a desert city into one with a stunning environment and a super-efficient government? I don't think so.

Dubai City does not have a particularly long history. Since it is located in an unbelievably harsh terrain, there have been very few battles fought there since no one wanted any part of this land! Dubai was founded in the year 1833 by Shaikh Maktoum Bin Buti Al Maktoum. In those early days the major occupation and source of livelihood of her inhabitants was fishing and pearl diving.

For many years, Dubai was just an obscure society somewhere in the Middle East. It was a society that had no streets, cars, running water, electricity, schools, hospitals, or infrastructure. But this was soon to change when oil was discovered just off the coast in 1966. Suddenly Dubai was rich beyond anyone's wildest imagination! It was like winning the lottery.

Over the course of just a few decades, Dubai has transformed from a sleepy little coastal village into a world-class city, famous for its ambition, drive, and economic promise. And guess what! It is all the result of one man's vision! Shaikh

Mohammed bin Rashid Al Maktoum.

In 1995, Shaikh Mohammed became the crown prince of Dubai with a chief objective of overseeing the transformation of this small patch of desert into the world's most luxurious resort and business destination.

On January 4, 2006, Shaikh Mohammed bin Rashid Al Maktoum became the ruler of Dubai as well as the prime minister and vice-president of the UAE. He was the tenth ruler from the Al Maktoum family lineage.

Shaikh Mohammed is reputed for having a distinctive and inviolable criterion for anything that concerns Dubai. The criterion is that everything Dubai must be "world class". By that, he means anything done in Dubai at all must be unprecedented in the world and "The Guinness Book of Records". Thus Dubai has a list of many first iconic achievement under her belt.

There are many things in Dubai today that carry the appellation of the longest, heaviest, highest, and biggest or the very best of anything ever in the world. This list includes the world's largest indoor theme park, which is the size of about 26 football fields that is completely enclosed and temperature controlled.

It's also home to the world's biggest ski dome. As well as a home to the world's first fully furnished underwater hotel – Hydropolis. The hotel has been touted to be the only 10-star hotel in the world!

Not forgetting the world's tallest tower, the Burj Khalifa, which stands at 2,717ft, an artificial archipelago – Dubai's man-made islands made in the shape of a palm tree amongst a host of other jaw-dropping architectural masterpieces.

This inviolable criterion of Shaikh Mohammed has helped him convert Dubai into something that looks more of a science fiction than real life reality.

How did Dubai do all these? For sure, they took the best

from all nations and then modified it to fit into their own scenarios. And that is exactly what we must do as Nigerians too. Let us gather all Nigerians in the diaspora. Let's put our heads and experiences together and create a masterpiece out of them.

Dubai achieved this in spite of the fact that the Middle East is famous for lots of conflicts, tensions and political instability. Yet she has gone ahead to become a political, economic and financial success. It is even adjudged one of the safest places in the world to live or to visit as a tourist because of the safety it has been able to provide to millions of tourists over the years.

To prepare for these roles, Shaikh Mohammed received a diverse education starting at an early age and was able to strike a balance as both a business leader and a political ruler thereby producing cultural, economic and social prosperity for the people of Dubai.

Through his initiative Dubai invested heavily in local construction when loans were cheap and made property investments abroad as the market was peaking. Before long, Dubai experienced a multiyear boom that turned it into an ultramodern city right in the middle of the desert.

In 2002, Mohammed issued a land reform decree allowing foreigners to own real estate in Dubai — a first in any Gulf state. Before the reforms, Dubai had no real estate market.

With the 2002 reform, anyone could buy a home in Dubai — an opportunity with particular appeal to wealthy families in unstable countries nearby.

Indians, Russians, Lebanese all poured cash into Dubai properties. It quickly became a hotbed for the wealthy barons of the Middle East, North Africa, South Asia and the former Soviet Union to pack their wealth into. Before long, it was named the world's fastest growing city with an astonishing array of modern architecture. Dubai experienced as much property development as Shanghai, a city with 13 times its population.

However, sometime late in the year 2008, around October or thereabout the world financial crisis struck Dubai's economy, slamming the brakes on its development. Projects that were in full swing were delayed and tourism declined greatly but Sheikh Mohammed introduced a brilliant strategy to lure multinational companies to the sheikdom.

It turned out to be a gem of an idea as many free zones were carved, each specifically designed to woo an industry he felt would benefit Dubai. Lured by the prospect of tax-free salaries, many of the international businessmen who visited Dubai never returned to their country for business. They stayed there, prospered and contributed to the making of Dubai.

Meanwhile, back in the 1980s, Mohammed had breathed new life into the languishing Jebel Ali port by declaring it Dubai's first 'free zone.'

Free zones in many countries were simply areas where companies were exempt from taxation. But in Dubai, there were no corporate or income taxes to begin with and Jebel Ali Free Zone was more like a Special Economic Zone in Deng Xiaoping's China, where separate laws applied within the SEZ than beyond the gates. Jebel Ali thrived under the new regime, becoming one of the busiest ports on the planet and helping Dubai become what it is today.

Sheikh Mohammed took up his good works a step further. He set up the Dubai International Finance Centre (DIFC) which is being referred to as a state within a state. It practices Western type of business. It has it's own court system presided over by an imported British judge, it's own official currency – the U.S dollars rather than the UAE dirham as well as it's own official language – English. The DIFC is home to major banking giants on the global scene including HSBS, Citibank, Standard Chartered and Credit Suisse.

And then Sheikh Mohammed also saw to the construction of Internet city and Media City. A 53 story twin Chrysler buildings standing next to each other. Internet city houses the

Middle East headquarters of Microsoft, Dell, Hewlett-Packard and Canon amidst others. While Media city houses the foreign bureau of Western News Media such as CNN, Reuters, BBC, as well as top Arabic stations such as al-Jazeera and al-Arabiya.

These are just few of the many inventions one man by the name Sheikh Mohammed brought to a small patch of desert located in an obscure place in the Middle East. As a result of the astonishing development that has taken place in Dubai, it is often compared to Singapore, Hong Kong, Orlando or even Las Vegas but many have avowed that the sheikdom is more like a hybrid of all them.

With all these in view, tell me again that only God can save Nigeria and I will tell you that you're the last joker of the century. Which offerings, seeds, sacrificial giving, speaking in tongues, sleeping in churches or prayer meetings did Sheikh Mohammed bin Rashid al-Maktoum and his people indulge in for them to have made Dubai the hub of civilization? None, absolutely none whatsoever.

So, friends; instead of folding your hands and looking to the supernatural to help transform Nigeria, stand up tall, take a stand and decide that you as an individual and a citizen of Nigeria will bring about the jaw dropping change that you desire for the nation.

> *"It is not in the star to hold our destiny but in ourselves"* (WILLIAM SHAKESPEARE)

The Dubai story is proof of what is possible if any nation decides for a change. It proves that any nation including our beloved Nigeria can actually become anything if they will get off their butts and do the work. Or do you think they did that because they are better than us? Do you think the odds were stacked in their favor? I don't think so. If anyone has an advantage at all, I must tell you that we are the ones who have the advantage.

Enough of the "only God can save Nigeria" mentality when people with little or no affiliation with God are doing great things. Enough of waiting for God when those who don't even know Him are busy creating wonders just by taking advantage of their rights to rule and dominate over the earth.

The truth is that whatever single invention that a godless nation comes up with, a nation of godly people like ours can do much more. So awake from your slumber oh ye Nigerians and let's turn Nigeria into a wonder for the world to see.

PART 3

Practical Steps to
a New Nigeria!

CHAPTER 9

God Is Waiting
For Sons

God Is Waiting For Sons

Have you ever been in a relationship with someone who only cared about what you can do for them without any consideration to what your needs might be? Or do you know someone who is only concerned about what they can get from you without bothering to be of any good to you?

My guess is that if you happened to be in a relationship with someone like that, you will probably take to your heels as fast as your legs can carry you. Yet, in our selfishness and immaturity, many of us only think about using God to meet our needs without really caring to find out if God on the other hand has needs that we can meet.

Yes I know you will say "but He is God, He can't need anything. Even if He has a need, it will take another God to meet His need not this little me" But that is where you are wrong my dear. God has a need and yes, you are capable of meeting that need!

God is in need of people who will say use me Lord, send me father, here am I send me. He is in need of people who will hear the voice of the cry of the masses and make themselves available to be used of Him. He is in need of people who will flow on the same frequency with Him for saving the nations of the world.

Trust me, Nigeria is on the mind of God big time. He sees the sufferings of the people and has heard their cry. But for reasons we both know, He can't step into the situation Himself. He needs to step in using you and me. He needs us to rise to the occasion so He can use us to get things done.

Listen my dear, the days of selfish thinking are long gone. God is tired of people who only come to Him for blessings for themselves and their immediate families. He is looking for people who will think national transformation. He is looking for people who will submit themselves to be used of Him in their area of passion. He needs someone whom He can send into the world of sports, someone He can send to the world of entertainment, business, industrial development, education and so on. He needs you and I to infiltrate our areas of influence and gifting with the kingdom life.

> "Also I heard the voice of the Lord, saying:
> "Whom shall I send, and who will go for us?
> "Then I said, "Here am I! Send me." (ISAIAH 6:8)

The ultimate question is: are you available? Are you available to be sent into the world of your passion and influence? Are you available to be sent into the world of your gifting or does God have to look for someone else?

Just in case, you are still wondering what in the world God needs you for, let me explain a bit.

> "And unto Adam he said, Because thou hast heark-
> ened unto the voice of thy wife, and hast eaten of
> the tree, of which I commanded thee, saying, Thou
> shalt not eat of it: cursed is the ground for thy sake;
> in sorrow shalt thou eat of it all the days of thy life;
> Thorns also and thistles shall it bring forth to thee;
> and thou shalt eat the herb of the field;" (GEN 3:17-18)

Following the sin and fall of man, God looked at him and pronounced the consequences of his action to him. I know many have said God cursed him but a careful look at this shows otherwise. God simply spelt out to Adam the consequences of his actions. He told him that the ground was cursed for his sake. In other words, because of what he had done, the ground (earth) had come under a curse!

As a result of the curse, the ground that should have ordinarily brought forth its fruit with ease was now going to be doing that with sorrow. This was the beginning of all of man's predicament. The ground that was designed to bring forth fruits after its kind was now conditioned to bring forth thorns and thistles.

Thorns and thistles represent all the hardships and difficulties of life. They represent all the maladies of human existence. Everything evil that man ever required to be saved from came as a result of the thorns and thistles that followed the sin of man in that Garden. Every single problem that is facing our beloved country Nigeria and every other nation on the earth right now is as a direct result of that curse.

Somehow, everything and everywhere that you can find earth (sand or ground) was now under a curse of hardship. It was this curse of hardship that translated into the various things that make life difficult and unbearable for us as humans. Things continued like that until the coming of Christ who through His death redeemed man from the curse.

Based on the works of Jesus, man was now exempt from the sin of the garden. However, the earth was not redeemed alongside man. The earth did not experience the new birth at salvation like we humans do. This is because God has a different program for the redemption of the earth. Since in the first place, the earth only came under corruption and bondage through the sin of man, it was proper for the salvation of the earth to be as a direct result of man.

So instead of just saying the earth was okay because man was saved, God designed for man to be the one to redeem the earth. God designed that the earth will only be saved through the deliverance that man brings to it. Thus, you and I became responsible for the deliverance of the world today. This again

GOD IS WAITING FOR SONS

is the reason why it is an insult of the highest order for us to turn around and chant that chorus that "only God can save Nigeria."

My question is: was it God that put Nigeria under bondage and corruption? The answer is "no". Every single problem we cry about today has a direct link with man. So whatever man has done to our country, man can undo as well. We shouldn't now wait for God to come and fix what we have created. Rather we should take up the responsibility to do just that.

This is the reason why God is looking out for deliverers today. He is not just looking for children but for children who have been trained into sons. He is looking for men and women who have been trained in the message that you are receiving now. He is looking for the mature sons who will say "here am I Lord, send me".

God needs people to say "here am I Lord send me into the world of business". He is eagerly waiting and looking for deliverers for every sphere, stratum, and institution of the nation. He needs people like you who would say: here am I Lord, send me into the world of the Nigerian politics. Here am I Lord, send me into the world of industrial development. Here am I Lord, send me into the world of economics." Whatever area of life you have been called into or are passionate about, God is looking for you to say "here am I Lord, send me".

You see, the only way the curse of the earth can be destroyed over the earth is when the sons of God take over the earth. We are the ones with what it takes to bring deliverance to the spheres of life that thorns and thistles have eroded. We are the ones with the answer to the cry of millions of Nigerians. Until God finds someone who is willing to be sent into a sphere of life, God cannot be involved with it. Until God has His sons in the various institutions of our nation, He cannot be involved with the change that we all cry for.

Remember that as His children, we are actually the carriers of God. We are His channels and out stretched arm of help. It is only when we go that God goes because He can only work through us. He needs to use our bodies. He needs to use our heads and minds. He needs to use your personal skills, gifts and passion to bring about a change in your area of calling but until you move, nothing will happen.

USE ALL YOU'VE GOT

One of the most remarkable personalities of the whole bible is the man named Moses. He played such a pivotal role in the life and history of the Israelites that we cannot afford to ignore him. He was a man that could have been described as being born at the wrong time but God spared his life for a purpose. God caused the same man who was after his life to take him in and raise him in the best way possible.

I mean he was a man whom God gave a unique opportunity to be raised in the palace of Pharaoh for a reason. That opportunity gave him the best education of his day. He was trained by the best but unknown to many, that was all for a purpose.

By making himself available, God used him to bring about a deliverance to the people of Israel. Listen, the Israelites were in bondage for over 400 years but God used one man to bring about their deliverance. Think what He can use you to do if only you will make yourself available! If only you will say, here am I, send me Lord!

Listen dear friend, there are opportunities that God has given you in life in order to better position you to bring the kingdom into those places. You have developed skills and expertise in certain areas that can be used to bring about the deliverance of nations in that sphere. The exposures you have and the experiences you have gathered over the years were all for the same reason. It's now time for you to put together all that you have acquired for the benefit of your calling and assignment. It is time you put your full weight into making sure that the area of the society that God has brought you up for does not suffer again.

You might be the Moses that we need in the telecommunications world. You might be the one with the deliverance for our banking system. You might even be the one to deliver the country from the monstrous hands of corruption, but as long as you do nothing, there will be no change. For as long as you sit and watch, things will move from bad to worse and from worse to worst.

You might be the Moses that we need in the world of Medicine, education, entertainment, commerce, business, finances, social. You might even be the Moses to the needy people, orphans or poor.

Imagine a country like ours with just 1 million deliverers! Imagine that we all found our places and went all the way bringing about deliverance there. Who will ever remember to say that only God can save Nigeria? God is calling out to you today saying "who shall I send?"

> *"A life is not important except in the impact it has on other lives."* (JACKIE ROBINSON)

Let me tell you a secret right now. If you ever felt like life wasn't as much fun as you would have loved it to be, it is because you have been spending your life doing the wrong things. When you set out like I am telling you to do now and commit your life to bringing about deliverance in a sphere of life that you are passionate about, life will take on a whole new meaning for you. Life will begin to make more sense to you.

Imagine the joy of being responsible for smiles and changes in the lives of one person, five people, ten people or even hundred people. Imagine waking up in the morning knowing that you had another 24 hours to make a difference for your generation and even generations to come.

"In every day, there are 1,440 minutes. That means we have 1,440 daily opportunities to make a positive impact." (LES BROWN)

HOW TO MAKE AN IMPACT IN THE WORLD

I have found that oftentimes, people are of the opinion that for them to really make an impact in life, they have to get to the moon, find a way to live on mars or make some "out of the world" scientific discovery! Yet, nothing can be farther from the truth than this.

Yes, there is the place of inventing something completely out of the world but that is not the only way to make a difference in the world. In most cases; we are better off starting by improving on what already exists. We are better off taking a cue from what is and making it better than it presently is.

So I will like to ask you, what is it in the Nigerian system today that you can improve on. What do you think you can make better for the benefit of the general public? Maybe, it is the traffic problem that you can come up with an idea to fix. It can be a tweak in our educational system that you can give birth to. Just think improvement!

As a matter of fact, most of those we celebrate around the world today did just that. Steve Jobs, Bill Gates, Henry Ford and so on. They didn't quite invent something that didn't exist but took their time and talent into making what existed better.

For example, many people around the world accredit the discovery of the electric light bulb to Thomas Edison while in reality, he never did! Don't let that surprise you. The electric bulb has been in existence for several years before Thomas Edison. The major problem was the fact that the version of electric bulb available then was unreliable, expensive and short-lived.

WHO INVENTED THE LIGHT BULB?

Sir Humphry Davy

Starting in the early 1800s, inventors looked for ways to convert electricity into light. Sir Humphry Davy, an English physician, successfully passed an electric current through platinum strips in 1801. Unfortunately, the strips evaporated quickly and Davy was unable to create a light that lasted more than a few minutes.

In 1809 Davy created what would become known as the Arc lamp. He made an electrical connection between two charcoal rods connected to a battery. The light from this was very bright but small.

Warren de la Rue

For the next 50 years, others sought ways to lengthen the amount of time the light source would remain. In 1840 Warren de la Rue, a British scientist, placed a platinum coil in a vacuum tube. When he passed an electric current through it, light was formed. This design was efficient and the light lasted longer, but platinum was very expensive which made it impossible to be distributed on a commercial level.

Frederick de Moleyns

In 1841 Frederick de Moleyns of England was given the first patent for an incandescent lamp. His design used powdered charcoal. He heated this material between two platinum wires in a vacuum bulb.

Joseph Wilson Swan

Joseph Wilson Swan was born in 1828 in England. He worked as a physicist and chemist. Swan wanted to produce a practical, long-lasting light source. He used a carbon paper filament in his light bulbs. In 1878 he received a British patent for his light bulb. Swan began placing light bulbs in homes throughout England. By the early 1880s he had started his own light bulb company.

Thomas Edison

While Swan worked in England, Thomas Edison was busy in the United States. He experimented with thousands of different filaments. His goal was to find materials that would light well and last for a long time. He brought in various metals and supplies from all over the world.

Then in October of 1879, Edison had a breakthrough. He carbonized a piece of sewing thread. Using this as a filament, he was able to produce a light bulb that burned for thirteen and a half hours. By bending the filament, he could make the lamp burn for over 100 hours. Eventually Edison invented a bulb that could glow for more than 1200 hours. He received a patent in 1880 for his light bulb. It had the same features of today's modern light bulbs: an incandescent filament in a glass bulb with a screw base.

The Real Inventor of the Light Bulb

You see, real invention isn't just about doing something new or doing something no one has ever done before. Real invention is taking what already exists and taking it to the next level. It is about perfecting something that existed before.

When the question is asked, who invented the light bulb, Joseph Swan and Thomas Edison are usually given credit. However, both of these men worked off of previous inventions. Historians estimate that over twenty inventors worked toward the creation and design of the light bulb. Of these, Edison's version was the most efficient.

By creating a vacuum inside the bulb, finding the right filament to use, and running lower voltage through the bulb, Edison was able to achieve a light bulb that lasted for many hours. This was a substantial improvement, and one that led with more improvements, to making the light bulb practical and economical.

So what Thomas Edison really did was to find a way to reduce the cost by making them with cheaper filaments that also lasted longer.

It is therefore appropriate to credit numerous inventors that lived during the 1800s. Even after Swan and Edison, others continued to improve the light source. The light bulb as we know it today, is a result of much time and effort. Remember that the next time you flip on the switch!

Why do I tell you all these? It is to help you see that there is a unique reason for your being here. It doesn't matter how many other people have been at that same venture, no one else can do it like you can. God needs you to bring in your unique and personal twist to turn our nation around for God. There is something about your personality that shines through the things you do that no one else can ever have. So don't say you are too little or insignificant.

Imagine that over twenty distinct efforts by other inventors all over the world were already underway when Edison entered the light bulb invention race. One would have thought he shouldn't bother since there were already others doing something in that line but no. he refused to settle because others were already doing it.

He went on to improve on what others had discovered and made a difference that the world cannot forget him for. Even though he wasn't necessarily the originator of the idea, the truth remains that he made it possible for the common man to have access to electric bulbs.

So don't you say your idea is not original. Don't you say that what you are called to do is common because there is no such thing as a common calling. You are uniquely designed to perform in a way no one else can and to get results no one else can. Therefore, your refusal to step up and do something with your calling means depriving the several billion people on earth an opportunity to have their lives improved in one way or the other.

Imagine that the man who was born with the invention of electricity in his DNA failed to do so. What do you think would be happening to the world right now? Where do you think we will all be today? In fact, it is very unlikely that you would have been able to read this book right now because the computer used to type it out is powered by electricity and so is the printer used to print it as well.

Let's stop waiting for God to come and change Nigeria when He already has us on board. Make up your mind not to fail our beloved country Nigeria!

IT'S TIME TO COOPERATE WITH GOD

By now you already know that as much as God would like to do something about the state of things in Nigeria, He is literally incapacitated without you and me. He can't do much without a human agent and that is where you come in. He wants to bring about deliverance and salvation to the various sectors of our nation's economy but He can only accomplish that through you and me. It is often said that:

"If a child doesn't raise his hand, you can't carry him. The child has to cooperate with you if you are going to carry him"

The same is applicable to God here. Except we cooperate with Him, there is little or nothing He can do to save Nigeria. Before God can save Nigeria, we must cooperate with Him. So it's time we began to cooperate with Him. It is time we began to respond to that call of God for a savior in our land. It is time we began to say: "here I am, send me"

Until God finds a man to say so, it doesn't matter how many times we cry and shout that "only God can save Nigeria", nothing will happen. It is you and I who will have to take God into the various sectors of the nation and introduce Him there. It is you and I who will have to bring hope again to our land by getting involved ourselves. While others are chanting and even praying that only God can save Nigeria, you and I would be making progress changing things in the affairs of our nation because we have said "here we are, send us"

In the coming chapters, I will be showing you how you can identify the areas of life that you have been called and designed to influence. I will show you what you should begin to do in that sphere of influence to bring about change and development there in no distant time. So come along with me and let's find out what mountains and spheres of the country you have been designed to fix for the common good of all.

CHAPTER 10

Let Sons Arise!

Let Sons Arise!

There are several people in our country who are of the opinion that they can never be of any relevance to national development because they aren't politicians. They think that only those elected into political offices have the opportunity to make a difference in the economy and the nation at large but this is so wrong. In fact, in some case, those elected into political offices have a much lesser chance of making a difference than those who aren't! This is because when elected into office, you come under the influence of several factors and can't really function on your own like those who aren't in office.

I am guessing that the question on your mind right now is "if people who aren't elected into political offices have a higher chance of contributing positively to national development, how are they supposed to do it?"

The answer is that this is why it is important for every one of us to discover our passion and place of assignment in life. Every one of us must find the sphere of influence that we feel passionate about making a difference in. And trust me, each of us has at least one; many of us have even more than one.

One of the beauties of finding your place of assignment in life is the fact that when you find it, you have found your own area of contribution to national development. You have found that thing you can do to contribute positively to the development of our nation. Therefore, you should stop thinking you can't do anything to improve things in the land because you are not a politician.

For example, let us say that you are passionate about the entertainment industry. You feel like that is where you have an input to make. That automatically becomes your own field of operation. That becomes the place where you should do something to improve the nation as a whole. Yes, you may not be the governor of the state or a senator but you are in a position that the governor can never be. Therefore, you can do something that the governor can't do.

What you should do therefore is begin to brainstorm on how you can bring about development to that sphere of life. How can you make the country better from the entertainment side of the matter? What can you do to make our entertainment industry better than it is now? A good place to begin is to find out the major problems and challenges of the industry right now. Then go ahead to find out ways to solve those problems for the industry. On the other hand, it might be something that is just okay in the industry that you think can move from just okay to great! The moment you find those out, you want to begin to strategize and plan towards taking it to the next level.

Now imagine that while you are doing that in the entertainment industry, someone else is doing the same in the industry of commerce and another is doing so in the police force. Imagine that with all that, someone else is doing something in our educational sector while another is doing so in the judiciary system and even in the medical sector. Can you see how we can take the destiny of the country into our hands and change it over a given period of time?

This is the reason why I say God is not looking for politicians. Rather He is looking for ordinary men and women who will take up the responsibility to bring about change, growth and development in their respective areas of influence. He is looking for simple individuals who will make up their mind to do extraordinary things in their sphere of life rather than sit and chant the chorus "only God can save Nigeria".

Hence, you must identify that area or sector of the land that you are passionate about fixing today. You must also begin from this moment to take steps towards bringing about salvation and deliverance in that sphere of operation. You must begin to confront the problems and challenges there. You must bring about change, growth, development and hope in the sectors of the land that you are concerned about.

Please stop waiting for the government and start doing something now. You don't necessarily have to change the whole country but you can start from one group or category of people that you are passionate about and take things up from there.

A CASE STUDY ON NATIONAL INFLUENCE FROM TATIANA

Let me tell you the inspiring story of a lady called Tatiana in our church. She was a drug addict and a prostitute who got transformed through our ministry in Ukraine. This lady had slept with more than a thousand men in the course of her prostitution. But thank God all that changed when she came in contact with the kingdom message that I preach.

While she was in school, she always felt abused by the attitude of the teachers and so she always fought them. She had been expelled from four different schools for fighting her teachers and that was when she finally dropped out of school.

As I would normally do with my mentees, I started by helping her identify her passions and area of calling. I helped her discover that God must have allowed her to have such a horrible experience back then in school so she could come back to be the deliverer in that sphere.

However, according to the law in Ukraine, the church is completely separate from the school. So it is not exactly possible to come to the school and say you want to teach them the bible or anything religiously inclined. In fact, you couldn't use school properties for any religious gathering or activity at all.

In addition to that, she was reluctant to do anything because she thought she didn't have anything to offer. She felt that she most likely wouldn't be accepted by the school because of her past reputation. So this was where the wisdom of God came in. We sat down with her to figure out how to do so.

I told her that she was already equipped for the task because of her story and testimony. The mere fact that she had changed from what she used to be to a responsible citizen was enough to get her a hearing I told her. I also added that the key to being an influence and penetrating into any sphere of life is to know that you are coming as an answer to a problem there.

I explained that when you provide an answer to people's needs, they begin to see you in a different light. They begin to see that they need you. So I asked her to start by writing down the problems she could identify that the schools were having.

Looking critically at her own life, she said her own problem started because of the wrong attitude of the teachers. They were disrespectful to her and she couldn't cope so she started fighting with them. Then I asked her if she thought the problem still existed in the schools today. I asked her if she thought teachers still push students into wrong habits because of their attitudes towards the students. Then she said of course. In fact it is even worse now than it was then!

I said "great, it means that the whole school system and the whole nation knows that there is a problem with teachers' attitudes to students" So that is going to be our bait for getting into the school. We are going to tell them that we are coming to solve this problem. We are going to tell them your story of how you became a drug addict and a prostitute and how these vices are linked to this attitude of the teachers. We would tell them you're coming to give back, then show them how your life has changed now and how they can stop the crisis between students and teachers.

Then I asked her what other problems the schools had. Then she said schools have issues knowing what to do with student truancy. So I said that is another point for us. We are going to tell them that we are coming to show them what to do with students. We will show them how to stop student truancy in the school.

She also talked about the problem of students smoking, drinking, missing out on classes and doing all sorts of things in and out of school. So at the end of the day, we came up with a list of several problems facing the schools. Then we turned the solution to all these problems into a teaching and training curriculum!

We came up with a program to teach: how to make students respect teachers, why students should honour their teachers, what students will gain from honouring their teachers and so on. The curriculum also included: why it's wrong to smoke, drink or use drugs, why students should discover who they are and more.

We got professional educators to organize and package the program to meet up with the educational standards and requirement of the country. Then she also went to the university to study education herself so she could have a base for being the educator of this program.

We started from the school she had been chased from. When they saw her and observed the change in her own life, they wanted to find out what happened so she told them everything and told them that she can help them. She introduced her program to them.

When we launched, we started in one school. As she shared her story and experience of how she was a drug addict and a prostitute who has slept with over 1000 men during her career as one, the students and teachers were captivated. In fact, some of the students who used to run away from mathematics and science classes were coming for her own classes. The teachers and students alike wanted to come for her classes because it was not just theories but real life teachings.

At the end of the day, the director of the school was so appreciative that they gave an appreciation letter to Tatiana. So she took that appreciation letter and approached another school in the city. Soon enough the school directors and principals from the schools she had taught started recommending other schools for the program.

To cut the long story short, the ministry of education got to know about it and adopted the program to be a compulsory program for all the high schools in the Kiev region! The government was now sponsoring the publishing of the book made out of the program and more than 300 schools were participating in the program.

Note that Tatiana didn't just sit there waiting for the government to do something about the educational sector of the country. She didn't even start by selling the idea to the government. She started locally. Did something on her own to bring about this change beginning from her own school. It was her result that got the attention of the government and eventually made it a national movement!

This is what it means to let your light so shine before men that they may see your good works and glorify your Father which is in heaven. This is what it means to be the light of the world. Tatiana demonstrated that she was the light of the world of education in her country and that brought about a much desired change.

What about you? What are you going to do? Which area are you going to take your light into? Which area are you going to shine so much that men will take notice of you? What are you going to do to improve the lives of others and by extension improve the state of things in the country?

I repeat that you don't need a government appointment or office to become an agent for national transformation. All you have to do is begin by finding out where you have been chosen to be the light and off you go shinning for men to see.

HOW TO SHINE IN THIS WORLD

One of the most popular but least understood concepts of the kingdom is that of us being the light of the world. Every now and then, we all chorus that we are the light of the world but very little do we really understand what that means. For the most part, all we have been taught to do is just to say it without ever caring to find out how we are supposed to shine. We never really get to be told how this light that we are should affect the world.

So what you find is that there are too many lights all clustered in one place (the church). Yet, the original purpose of the light has always been for the illumination of the world. Light has always been designed to be appreciated only in the dark. It is only out there in the world where there is darkness and even utter darkness that the light is actually useful.

Hence, my idea that the church shouldn't be a place where lights just gather to have some nice and cool feeling. It should be a breeding ground where people are trained to identify the particular darkness in the world and our nation in particular they have been called to fix.

But thank goodness, God didn't leave any stone unturned in showing us how we are to be the light of the world. He made sure He made it crystal clear enough for us to grasp.

> *"Ye are the light of the world. A city that is set on a hill cannot be hid. Neither do men light a candle, and put it under a bushel, but on a candlestick; and it giveth light unto all that are in the house. Let your light so shine before men, that they may see your good works, and glorify your Father which is in heaven."* (MATT 5:14-16)

Dear friend, did you know that right about this moment, you are that city that has been set upon a hill and cannot be hid? Did you know that you are that candle that has been placed on a candlestick to give light unto all that are in the house? Why then are you crying and complaining about the darkness around? Why have you joined the bandwagon of those who claim that "only God can save Nigeria"? Why are you just finding one excuse or the other to give as to the reason why there is still darkness in the various sectors of our nation?

Imagine that there was a bulb in your house and when you turn the bulb on at night, you hear a sound "only God can light this room" from the bulb! How would that make you feel? How would that sound to you? Chances are that the next thing you will consider doing would be replacing that bulb with a bulb that would do what it is there for.

Sadly, this has become the state of things in our country Nigeria. Those who should have been in offices, factories, laboratories, libraries and other places doing productive work have all been locked up in churches and mosques. We have all allowed religion and religious activities take the place of the necessary work for the development of our land. We have abdicated our responsibility all in the name of "only God can save Nigeria". What a myth we have believed all this while!

The problem I see here is that many of us have never been taught the latter part of this scripture. We haven't been told that our light is designed to shine in our immediate environment and society rather than in the church or mosques. Our light is designed to light up our society in such a manner that men should take notice of us. We should be so effective that it becomes impossible for us to go unnoticed.

This is why I say you don't have to wait for the government to change things. You don't have to wait for the government to lay down policies to help you get things done. You don't need an allocation from the state bursary either. All it takes is each and every one of us being in our unique places of calling and shinning the light there. All it takes is for every single one of us to ensure that he is shining so well that he draws both national and international attention!

Listen closely friends, it is in your sphere of influence that you are supposed to shine as light. It is in your domain and area of concern that you are supposed to shine.

Come on here, don't you know that you can shine so much in the world of banking that bankers begin to take notice of you? You can become such an influence in the banking world that the authorities of the banking world would begin to notice you in a very special way. Soon enough, your influence would begin to affect policies and decisions that are made in that field. And finally, you would find that what started as a one man show has become a national movement.

CHAPTER 11

Identify Your Own Mountain

Identify Your Own Mountain

Very shortly, I will be showing you the various mountains we must rise up to take care of in our nation Nigeria. But just before I get into itemizing them, let me take a moment to explain what I mean by mountains.

It is a term derived from a statement made by Caleb in the bible. Sometimes in the course of their journey towards the Promised Land, Moses sent out twelve men to spy that land and bring reports about what sort of land it was. They were to tell everyone what the place looked like. When they returned, ten of the twelve men came with a discouraging report of how impossible it is to take over the land. They came with reports of how incompetent and inferior they were before the giants that dwelt in the land at that time.

These ten are like the majority of Nigerians today who only know of how enormous and insurmountable the problems of Nigeria are. They kind of have a magnifying lens on that only increases the size of the problem and makes them look so small and irrelevant in the scheme of things. The ten are like the Nigerians who have completely lost every iota of self-esteem and self-value left in them and are now of the opinion that they are too insignificant to make a difference in the affairs of the land.

But then, there were these other individuals who saw things differently. Their names are Caleb and Joshua. Though they saw the same things the other ten spies saw, their interpretation of the situation was completely different. They saw things just the way I am seeing them right now concerning Nigeria. They saw exactly what I am seeing and trying to get you to see too. They saw that there were giants in the land but they also saw that they were well able to take on the challenge. They saw that even though there was an opposition ahead, they were well fitted to handle the situation.

Oh how I wish that the Nigerian populace will see from this point of view as well. How I wish that we will all see that we are well able to take on those giants and mountains of problems that have befallen our beloved nation all these while. Oh that we will begin to see that God has already equipped us with the solution and answers to all the troubles. This is why I am writing to you right now. This is what I want you to see.

I want you to understand that as a nation, we are well able to handle the challenges of the day. We have the capacity to deal decisively with every problem that has befallen our country. We have all that it takes to keep things under perfect control in our land. And it is time we began to do something in this regard.

Caleb looked at the same mountain that the other spies saw and said "give me this mountain!" He said "give me this mountain and all the giants there" and I will drive them away.

Come on somebody! What boldness and audacity this man is demonstrating here! This is exactly what we need in Nigeria my friends. This is what we should be saying and doing as individuals in Nigeria right now. Someone should be looking at the mountain of corruption and saying "give me this mountain and the giants therein". Someone else should be looking at the mountain of poor medical care in our country and saying "give me this mountain". You might have to look at the mountain of poverty and say "give me this mountain" as well.

Whatever mountain of problem befalling our dear country today that you feel called or passionate to solve, it is time to say "give me this mountain" as well. It is time to look the problem in the face and say I will bring you down. I will bring about change and development in this place. I will ensure that our country moves forward as far as this condition is concerned. And trust me when I say you can do it.

I am not just telling you a bunch of theoretical stuffs without any proof of results. These same principles I am sharing with you are the principles I have put to work in our church here in Kiev. They're the principles that have helped me to raise a church whose members make up 34% of the city's parliament. The same principles helped me to raise a church with over 3000 NGOs that are devoted to solving one problem in the society or the other. So I know exactly what I am talking about and I can guarantee that they will definitely work for Nigeria as well.

VARIOUS MOUNTAINS IN NIGERIA

Frankly speaking, the mountains of problems that have to be solved in our country cannot be described exhaustively in a single book. But what I am going to do here is to give you a general idea of these areas with some examples as well. That way, you have a foundation from which to begin to consider what you might have been called to do for Nigeria.

The fact remains that God is short of responsible men and women whom He can send to these spheres of life and influence. He is counting on you and me to do something about them. This is the reason I wrote this book. I have already found out my role and am well on the way to doing something about that but what about you? I am here to challenge you to respond to that cry of the Father for someone to send into the various sectors and areas of life in our dear country. I am here to challenge you to say "here am I, send me".

The Mountain Of Politics:

Even though I began with this, I don't want you to mistake it to mean that this is the most important area where God needs you and I to take charge. God is looking for sincere men he could send to politics to manage politics for Him. He is looking for people who will rise up to say "enough is enough" for the politics of our country. He is looking for people who will rise to the occasion to ensure that politics in Nigeria is run like it should.

Maybe, you are personally concerned about the political sphere of things in Nigeria. Maybe you sense that God is calling you to go into politics to represent Him and bring about change and development there. Now is that time to set to work. Now is the time to get off your high horse and begin to do something about it.

You may not exactly be called to run for political offices but to influence other aspects of the political world. You might be the one to implement an electoral system that will be truly free and fair across the country. It might be your idea that will re-educate the Nigerian populace on the importance of voting.

I once heard of a certain politician whom on the day of election gathered youths in their numbers in his house. These young chaps had come to receive instructions on how to go and maneuver things out there at the polling boots. As he instructed them and distributed arms to them, his children came out of the house. He enquired where there were going and they said they were going to vote. You won't believe what the man told his children that day!

He told them not to bother going to vote. He said it wasn't necessary because their votes wouldn't count or make any difference. He then added that it wasn't safe out there for them to go out. That was when it dawned on one of the youths there that the man never had their interest at heart. He wondered that the man wouldn't let his children out of the house let alone cast their votes but he was engaging the services of other people's children to disrupt the peace of the society.

Perhaps, you are the one to develop a program for young people that will teach them how not to allow themselves to be used as political bulldogs by all these power hungry politicians in our country. There are indeed several things we could possibly do to improve the way things are done in our political sphere of life and God is counting on you to make some of those changes.

The Mountain Of Business:

Let's face it, our business world is still somewhat backward compared to the way businesses are run in other parts of the world. That is why God needs men and women to send into that sphere to make a difference there. God is looking for sons to send to the world of business to manage it for him.

You might be the one that will get in there and change the way things are run. You might be the one that will bring about the development and growth in our business world. It might just be a program you develop that will help create a new breed of businessmen in our country. You can develop a system that will bring integrity back to our business world and change the international reputation of our dear country.

The economic history of presently developed countries like America, Russia, Japan and so on tends to support the fact that the economy is an "effect" for which entrepreneurship is the "cause."

The crucial role played by the entrepreneurs in the development of the Western countries has made the people of under-developed countries too much conscious of the significance of entrepreneurship for economic development. Now, people have begun to realize that for achieving the goal of economic development, it is necessary to increase entrepreneurship both qualitatively and quantitatively in the country. It is only active and enthusiastic entrepreneurs who fully explore the potentialities of the country's available resources – labour, technology and capital.

You might have a burden for entrepreneurship or entrepreneurial skills development in the country. You could set up an organization to teach, train and support up and coming entrepreneurs in their pursuits.

It's just like the story of Ojuloge Arts Ponmile, the CEO of Ojuloge ARTS World. Out of a burning desire to be of service to youths around her, she started an organization that catered for the needs of youths. She would organize conferences and symposiums training them to identify and maximize their talents. It wasn't long before the Lagos State government took notice of what she was doing and even gave her an award.

Now, she works hand in hand with the state government in hunting for talents within the state.

You can start up something that will meet a need or two around you. You might just be the next Ojuloge Arts Ponmile that our country needs.

The Mountain Of The Financial World:

What about our Banking industry? God is desperately looking for people to send to the world of finances to subdue it for Him. Will He find you? Can He send you to go and make a difference in the banking world? Can you come up with an idea or a project to turn our banks from just institutions that keep people's money to institutions that actually empower citizens for national development?

We need someone to get out there and do something to make our banks strong again. We need new banks to emerge with new ideas and new hope for the people of Nigeria. We need more customer friendly policies to be made in our banks and financial institutions. Someone has got to do something to stop the endless queue in our banking halls. And it will take someone like you to make these happen.

God is looking for sons to arise to the challenges of the financial institutions. In fact, chances are that you are more acquainted with the problems in that sector if you work or have an experience there. So who is a better fit than you in fixing the issues? Start thinking critically and creatively. Ask yourself "what can I do to make things different in this sphere? How can I contribute to the improvement of something that is not in best shape here?" these questions will get your creative juices flowing and I guarantee that ideas will begin to flow.

The Mountain Of Tourism:

Like I said earlier, many of us travel and holiday in other parts of the world that we admire. During our stay out there, we identified with certain things there that we enjoyed so much. In fact, there is a reason why we keep going back to those places as often as we have the opportunity to. What stops us from doing the same in our country? What stops us from making our own Nigeria a tourist center for the rest of the world? Who says we can't get the world's eyeballs on us if we set our minds to it?

God is looking for sons to send into the tourism sphere of our country. He is looking for men and women who will take the initiative to make our country a destination for the rest of the world. Needless to say is the economic development that becoming a tourist attraction center can bring to us. Imagine the number of jobs that will be created and the enormous amount of wealth that will be generated from our hotels and other sectors of the economy.

To put things in the right perspective, according to the World Tourism Organization, 689 million people travelled to a foreign country in the year 2000 spending more than $478 billion! The International Tourism Receipts combined with passenger transport currently total more than $575 billion – making tourism the world's number one export earner, ahead of automotive products, chemicals, petroleum and food.

What stops us from earning a portion of all that money? What stops us from being the world's choice destination?

The Mountain Of Education:

Another very important area that we have to begin to look into as a people is our educational system. Sometimes I am tempted to say that what we have right now is so far from being an educational system. That is why God is looking for prepared men to send to the world of education to manage the place for him. He is looking for experts and people with a burden for the way education is run in our country.

It is appalling to know that in this age and time, Nigeria still has a literacy rate of only 50% and of that 50% many of them were trained in the dilapidated schools and universities that we have today. Things have got to change and you are the one to bring about that change. God needs someone to come up with a way to ensure that quality education is first and foremost accessible to all people of all class. We must find a way to ensure that every Nigerian has access to good education no matter what.

Or how else do we demonstrate our hope and faith in the future if we will not do anything to train and educate the next generation? How else do we expect our economy to get better when we are not even maximizing the potentials of the human resources at our disposal as a nation?

I was surprised and shocked to my bone marrow when I heard of a family where the father doesn't believe in educating female children! And this was not some ten, twenty or thirty years ago. This was in 2016! Yet, the man has six daughters.

Shouldn't someone arise with a solution to cases like this? Shouldn't someone come up with a strategy to help such girls gain an education? God is definitely looking for people like you to take up this responsibility. He is looking for someone who will say "enough to discrimination against female children". And I am trusting that the person to do it is you.

You might not be able to send all female children to school by paying for their studies but you can set up an organization that sensitizes the public about this situation and I guarantee you that soon enough, funds will begin to flow.

I must praise the efforts of some of the states in the Niger-Delta region for placing their people on scholarships around the world. I must also praise the likes of Governor Rauf Aregbesola of Osun State for stepping into the crisis in the state and sending several of the students abroad on scholarship.

While scholarships are good and welcomed in our society, we must also consider developing our schools to become world class. We can also build international universities that other nationalities can apply to and aspire to study in. It is our call together to make that happen.

Even the learning conditions in the schools we have now have to be improved. Someone has got to come up with a plan to do that. Someone has got to develop a strategy to give our students a better learning environment in their schools.

I learnt of a certain young boy growing up in Lagos several years ago. While in primary school, he was so brilliant that his parents decided he should try the common entrance examination from Primary 5. But because of the policy of his school, he wasn't allowed to write the exam in his school. So his parents enrolled him to write the exam in another school. Though a primary 5 pupil, he had the best result in the school he enrolled to write the exam and got an admission to study in two Federal Government Colleges.

However, because he was not even ten yet, his parents were reluctant to have him leave for the boarding school just yet. So they found a secondary school in the neighbourhood and enrolled him as a day student. With each academic term, the boy's performance gradually deteriorated. His parents didn't read much meaning to that, they just thought it was because he was still young and finding it difficult to cope. They believed his performance will improve until one day, he returned home with a letter from the school summoning his parents to school the next day.

When his dad got there at around 10am in the morning, he was surprised to see almost all students outside and playing. He thought they were on break but when he enquired, he discovered they weren't on break. As a matter of fact, that was the norm in that school from morning till they closed at 2 pm.

Upon arrival in the office of the principal, he discovered that he had been summoned because his less than 12 year old son was found gambling with a few others in class the previous day. They were to be expelled from school and that was why they sent for the parents.

The man couldn't believe what he was hearing. He tried so hard to convince himself that it wasn't his bright son they were talking about but lo and behold, it was. Further enquiries revealed that his boy hasn't really been studying in that school. He daily routine in school was: resume, drop bag in class, run off to the field, go and eat during break, come back to class to rest and then find some indoor games to play.

The straw that broke the Carmel's back was when at the end of that term, the boy came back with a report card showing he was 118th position in a class of 128 students! The father knew he had to do something quickly or the future of his brilliant son would be ruined!

He quickly arranged and sent his son to another school where the learning condition was better. By the end of the first term in the new school, the boy was first position again! When he wrote the Junior WAEC that year, he was the best in his new school. And from that moment onwards, he was always placed in the first position until he finished secondary school. In fact, by the time he was in SS2, he had written GCE and passed all his papers. And then in SS3 he crowned it all by passing his final exams with 7 distinctions!

What made the difference in this boy's life was the quality and condition of schools he attended. Whereas he had been turned into a truant and gambler in one school, his potentials were greatly harnessed in another school. Only God knows how many destinies have been altered because of the learning conditions of our schools. Only God knows how someone who would have been a responsible citizen and bring about great change and development in the country might have been trained into a tout for going to a supposed school.

Maybe you are an educator or someone that has interest in education, I am challenging you to do your part to ensure that every child you have access to be raised and trained properly. If you are a school owner, I challenge you to look beyond your pocket and ensure that you are employing qualified teachers and educators there. Stop employing quacks who only make things worse for everyone at the end of the day.

God is looking for someone to bring about a solution to cultism in our universities. He is looking for someone that can bring about a ground breaking strategy to curb this cankerworm that have eaten so deep into our universities today. It is my hope that you who are reading this now will be that person to say "here I am, send me into the educational sphere"

The Mountain Of Art And Culture:

It is heart rending to know that our beloved country Nigeria still doesn't have a national identity we can all be proud of after so many years of existence. Little wonder why outside, others don't have much regards for us as a people. Instead of us to foster a unified national identity, what we have are tribalistic people who create trouble everywhere.

Whether Yoruba, Igbo or Hausa, the fact remains that we all have just one country. We are Nigerians for crying out loud! But what is the Nigerian culture? What can we say is the Nigerian way of doing things that we can all be proud of?

God is desperately looking for those he could send to the world of art and culture, to rule the place for him

The Mountain Of Entertainment:

Oh how my heart goes out to the entertainment industry in Nigeria! While we must admit that we are already coming up in the international realm of things when it comes to entertainment, the truth remains that our entertainment industry hasn't been effective in nation building. God is looking for gifted people to send to the world of entertainment, to reveal himself there.

When was the last time you listened to a Nigerian artist and felt so motivated to pursue your dreams or to make something significant of your life? When was the last time you watched a Nigerian music video and felt so inspired about your life that you got up and went in pursuit of your life's assignment?

Check out history and see what role Hollywood played in the great depression years in America. See how they cleverly used Hollywood to re-educate and inspire the entire country right in the middle of their trials.

Whereas, many were losing their jobs and many were jobless, the people still found their way to the theatres en masse during those days. But why was this so? It was because the movie industry performed a valuable psychological and ideological role, providing reassurance and hope to a demoralized nation! Even at the Depression's most dire moments, 60 to 80 million Americans attended the movies each week, and in the face of doubt and despair, films helped sustain national morale.

We must begin to do same with our movie industry in Nigeria. Our movies have got to become more educational than just a baseless show of rituals everywhere. This is the 21st century for crying out loud. We should be able to offer much more.

I am looking forward to producers that will emerge with movies of possibilities for the Nigerian populace. I am looking forward to movies that people will finish watching and get up to take the bull by its horns and bring about deliverance and salvation in their sphere of contact and influence.

What stops us from producing movies that a school dropout will finish watching and decide to go back to school? What stops us from producing movies that our kids will watch and be inspired to study even harder? Who says we can't produce movies that armed robbers and prostitutes will watch and have a total change of mind? It's all about coming up with the right concepts. And I am convinced that someone reading this book right now, will arise to the challenge and do this for our beloved nation.

The time has come for our musicians and other people in the entertainment industry to rise up to the occasion that the nation has found itself. It is time for worthy role models to emerge in our entertainment industry. I may not be a musician but someone reading this right now is.

My challenge to you therefore is to begin to think of how you can do something about the industry to move her forward. Begin to strategize about how the entertainment industry can become a major contributor to the development and health of the land.

It is high time someone came up with a lasting solution to piracy in Nigeria. Someone has got to do something decisive to stop these pirates and give our entertainers real value for their talents. You might just be the one to take Nollywood from where it is right now to Hollywood standard and beyond.

Enough of "only God can save Nigeria", when we are all here. Now is the time to arise, take up the responsibility and contribute our respective quotas in making our nation great again.

The Mountain Of Media:

Think about media in Nigeria and you think about an almost non-existent part of the economy. Imagine how backward and underdeveloped most of our media outlets are in this day and time. Yet there are many of us who have gone to the university to study about these things and come out with great ideas.

Why should BBC and CNN be the first to report events that occur in our very own borders? Why should Nigerians depend on other networks for facts about occurrences around us? Why must our media house and centers be known for only publishing malicious things about people? Is that our idea of professionalism or what? Aren't there capable people to handle these sectors in our dear country? I believe there are.

Many of our own have great ideas, degrees and the professional expertise to run media centers and yet, our media is nothing to write home about. Someone has got to arise to tackle the inefficiency of our media outlets. Someone has got to put a stop to the unhealthy manner that our media personnel have carried themselves. It is only in Nigeria that we glorify evil reports and slander good ones! But this has got to stop.

God is looking for journalists who will emerge with a dream to promote the nation rather than slander and bring it to disrepute. You can take it upon yourself to ensure that every simple effort that Nigerians make is publicized in such a way that will begin to cause a change in our public image as a nation.

Dear friends, God is desperately in search of sons and daughters he could send to the media world to reflect Him there. He needs you to bring in your professionalism and skills into the development of our media sector. He needs you to say "here I am, send me into the world of media."

The Mountain Of Sports:

Gone are the days when we hoped that we would go to the Olympics and came back with any significant medal. Gone are the days when Nigeria was known for her sportsmanship and all. But I ask. What stops us from producing champions in all spheres of sports?

God is desperately in search of those sons he could send to the world of sports to take care of things for him. He is looking out for someone like you who would say "here I am Lord, send me into the world of sports." But will that person be you?

Don't say you don't have a sponsor. Don't say no one is noticing you or no one knows you. If you will start from where you are and make a commitment to give your best at all levels, it won't be long before you are identified. Every athlete who ever represented the country was found somewhere doing something and it was definitely not in a prayer meeting!

You might have a calling as the coach or the trainer that Nigeria has been looking for all these years. You might be the one to prepare the Super Eagles to win the world cup one in the coming years. But sadly, that will never happen if you never step out. You have to find that place you are passionate about in this country and go all out to deliver the solution you carry inside you.

Even our churches can begin to do something about these things now. We can start up our own football clubs or sports centers and train people for these competitions. If our country must stand tall as the giant of Africa and indeed the giant of the world, we must all get involved. All hands must be on deck to make it happen and that is why I am challenging you to find your own place right now.

The Mountain Of Family Values:

The role and importance of the family in nation building is one that can never be over emphasized my dear friend. Most of the failures in our societies today are a direct link to a failure in the home front. Sometimes we find children who should have grown up normally and become agents of change and development in the country grow up with low self-esteem and other social complexes just because of the family they came from.

It is a known fact how family squabbles affect the developmental stages of children and churn out adolescents and youths who are more of problems to the society than solutions.

Did you know that every prostitute on the street came from a family? Every armed robber was born into a family as well. The educated ones who grew up to start stealing with their pens were also born into a family. The young people engaging in all manner of internet scams and giving our country a bad reputation were also born into a family. And psychologists have proven that what a child will become is largely dependent on what values are inculcated into them between the third trimester of pregnancy and their seventh year of life.

Based on that, wouldn't it be right to say that most of these people turned out the way they did because our families failed? Wouldn't it be appropriate to say that if the families had fulfilled their functions, our streets would have been safer today?

This is why God needs someone to send to the families. He needs someone to get up and begin to fix up the issues facing our families today. We need to drastically reducing the rate at which marriages fail in our nation. We need to stop the abuse of children who should be the future of our country. And who else to do this other than you?

You know deep down inside you how you are passionate and concerned for family values. You know you can do something to help fix our homes but there you are, doing nothing. At the very best, you are probably praying and asking God to take control of the families in Nigeria. But I say no! A thousand times no! Praying alone is far from being enough. Saying that only God can save the families in Nigeria is far from being correct. That wouldn't change a thing friends. That is why I am encouraging you to get up and do something right now.

Set up an organization to look into these matters and bring about the solution that we need. Find a creative way to educate and train couples. Begin to provide counselling services and all that to people at a rate they can afford. Whatever you can, do something to make a difference in our homes.

The Mountain Of Religion:

In the beginning of this book, I painted the picture of how we are such a religious country today. I showed how we spend countless number of hours and days in devotion to religious services but not much of that has translated into national development.

It is not because I am against religion per say. It is just that I think that all our devotion to religion hasn't delivered a commensurate result. And that is because we haven't done justice with what we teach and propagate in our places of religious activities.

When will people go to church or mosque and come back stirred to take up responsibility for a problem in the land? When will people go to church and discover the sphere of life they are supposed to dominate for God? When will church stop being about just what we do within the walls of the church? This is why I talk about the church without walls. The church that will not seclude itself from the society within which it functions.

Brothers and sisters, God is calling for a change. He is calling for a new breed of pastors, religious leaders and ministers to arise. He is calling for us to return to the message of national development rather than personal aggrandizement. It is high time we became more kingdom minded than self-minded my people.

God is in need of godly servants to send to the religious world to bring back his kingdom there. And my questions to you is: will He find you? Are you available or are you running your own agenda?

CHAPTER 12

Start Doing Something Now!

Start Doing Something Now!

Even though I've lived in Europe for the past 30 years of my life, I do interact with other Nigerians. As such I have come to realize that there are really several reasons why many of them are of the opinion that only God can save Nigeria. While the majority is mainly because of a lack of knowledge and laziness, there are still some who hold this opinion for other reasons. For some of these people, the reason they have resigned to fate and are waiting on God to come and save Nigeria is because they have come to believe that the Nigerian problem is above the capacity of man to solve.

Hence, after a long diatribe between these people and some other people they are discussing the problems of Nigeria with; they conclude with the statement – Only God can save Nigeria. Even, when it is on social media they highlight the malady facing the Nigerian nation, they still conclude – Only God can save Nigeria.

Sometime ago, I was privy to the discussion between two young chaps as they deliberated on the state of things in our beloved country Nigeria. The focus of their dialogue was that there might just be something spiritual about Nigeria that precludes anyone from being able to proffer solutions to her problems. They went ahead to say that every four years, Nigerians throng the polling booths to elect their politician of choice in hopes that he would come into power and make magic happen. They had high hopes that these men and women will be the messiah they have been looking for all along. Well for decades now, this hasn't proven true.

For decades Nigerians haven't been able to find those men who will come into power and spearhead the growth and development they have always dreamt about. As such those chaps began to wonder whether there might be some spiritual force obstructing the politicians from doing what they promised to do for the country before they got into power. And this is exactly what one of the discussants said:

> *"There is something about Aso Rock that makes anyone who sits there forget whatever dreams he had before he came in. Hence, we must now look up to God to help us fix our country."*

While I completely understand their frustrations, I still express that this is ignorance gone on rampage. This is a manifestation of the wrong mentality that has literally held our country bound all these while. The average Nigerian has come to believe that the responsibility of building a nation lies in the hands of those elected into political offices. They have been trained to believe that only those with access to public funds have the responsibility to do something about the nation while the rest of us just sit back and watch but nothing can be farther from the truth. Nigeria will only be built by Nigerians my dear friend!

GOD IS LOOKING FOR YOU, NOT THE GOVERNMENT

When it comes to building a nation, we must all understand that nations are not built by political office holders neither are they built by the government. I mean no matter who sits in the seat of power, no real development or change will happen to a nation by virtue of the person sitting there. It is the citizens of the land that will build the land. It is you and I who will build up our country.

Therefore, I am calling on all Nigerians to have a mindset shift. I am calling on all Nigerians to change their stand on this matter. I am calling on us all to stop bequeathing our right and responsibility in nation building to the government. It is time for us as Nigerians to rise to the occasion and build the Nigeria of our dream. It is time for us to wake up from our slumbers of many decades and face the challenge of our days.

Nigerians are some of the smartest and brightest people on the face of the earth today. All over the world, Nigerians have been involved in several processes that brought about the development and building of various societies. Nigerians have been pivotal to great inventions and discoveries all over and yet, we sit back and wait for the government to fix things for us. No, no, no. A thousand times no. It is time we stood up and took our places as individuals and did something remarkable for our land. After all, that is why we have brains!

Listen closely, when God said He made us in His image and likeness so we could look like and function like Him, He meant it. So guess what? Among other things, God is a creator!

That must mean that He has put some of that creative ability in you. He has made you a creator of some sort. As a matter of fact, you are a creator in your own capacity. God as a creator has made all the raw materials we would ever need available to us. He has ensured that all that is necessary for us to function as creators is in place because He is the only one with the ability to create out of nothing. But now that the materials are out there, we are the ones to take creation another step further.

Look at it this way, God never made a chair. Instead, He made the trees and we took it up from there. God never made cloths like we have them today. He rather made cotton and we took it up from there. He didn't give us petrol but He made the crude oil and we took it to the next level. What about the juice you drank today, was it God that made it? He only gave us water and we transformed it ourselves. You are probably wearing a shoe right now. Did God make that too? I don't think so. He just gave us animals and we turned their skin into leather and then into shoes and other things. So by all means, you are a creator and producer in your own capacity.

Every single Nigerian on the face of the earth, whether home or abroad is a bundle of solutions. We all came into this world fitted with all that it will take to fix at least one of Nigeria's many problems. My question to you therefore is: which problem did you come to fix?

Something interesting about man as a creator is the fact that all it takes for man's creative juices to start flowing is for him to have a problem! The presence of a problem plus critical thinking is what equals invention!

So never allow yourself to be overwhelmed by the enormity of the challenge before us as a nation. Never say that the problem of Nigeria is too big and cannot be solved. In reality, problems are a necessary resource for the release of our geniuses. Problems are the raw materials with which we create stuff. Problems get our creative juices flowing and bring out the best in us. For example, it was the problem of not having where to sit that resulted in the creation of chairs. The problem of slow means of transportation gave rise to the airplane too. The problems of Nigeria are a catalyst for our creative ability. So I ask again, what problem of the country are you going to take responsibility for right now?

You see, when I talk about identifying your mountain, I am talking about identifying that area of life where you have been called to be an influence. I am talking about pointing out a problem of the country for which God should not be bothered again. I am talking about taking the responsibility to fix something whether or not the government has a plan for it. I am talking about taking the initiative to do something specifically to bring about a change in at least one area.

Which of Nigeria's problems do you intend to match with your gifts, talents and brains? Isn't it time you came up with an idea that can create millions of jobs for people? What about coming up with an idea that will solve the problem of heavy traffic on our roads? Who says you can't invent something that will drastically improve the state of medical care in our beloved country? Why don't you develop that training program that will re-orientate our young people and prepare them for a successful and vibrant life?

There is at least one solution to the problems of Nigeria in you right now and it is time you started doing something to bring it forth. I challenge you to get off that chair. I challenge you to come out of your comfort zone. I challenge you to start thinking critically about what difference you can make as an individual in the affairs of our beloved nation. Start thinking about something significant you can do to change the lives of people in our motherland.

YOU DON'T HAVE TO REINVENT THE WHEEL

They say "travel and see" and truthfully, many of us have travelled and seen. Many of us Nigerians have had the opportunity to travel far and wide. We have been to developed nations and societies of the world. We have been to societies where things work at their optimal performance and have even seen how things work there.

What stops us from replicating some of what we have seen in those places in our own country? What stops us from reproducing the results we see and admire in those places? Yes, you may not be able to effect that change across the entire nation just yet but why not start from your own area of influence? Why not set up policies and structures in your own domain so things can function rightly there?

You have seen the high maintenance culture in Europe and other parts of the world, so why don't you implement that in your establishments as well. Why not set up a policy in your company that binds everyone who works there and prevents people from littering up the place?

What happened to the days when students in primary and secondary school were taught to pick up litter on the floor and put them in designated places even if they were not the ones that dropped them in the first place? Imagine that everyone who passed through our secondary schools came out with the mindset of picking up litter when they found them. Wouldn't we live in a much cleaner society? If you are a principal or owner of a school why not make that a policy in your school?

You have seen how women are protected in other parts of the world but when you come back home, you treat women like they are some piece of trash in human form. Don't you know that you might just be the one to bring about a whole revolution in an area of our society?

I can never forget the instance of a certain gentleman who travelled to Dubai on holiday a few years ago. He said as they drove out of the airport and to the hotel, he noticed that he didn't find any potholes at all. He quickly assumed that it must be the route they took. So the next day, he got his tour guide to take him around but go through an entirely different route from the one that leads to the airport. To his amazement, he noticed again that there weren't any potholes. He did that for the entire 2 weeks of his stay but never saw a pothole.

His joy knew no bound when he returned to Nigeria. He kept singing the praises of Dubai to everyone and anyone who was willing to give him an audience. He marveled that there was a city in the world where you could drive around for 14 days and not find a single porthole!

Who says we can't build cities like that? Who says we can't replicate those in our country? Isn't it because God decided to save Dubai and leave Nigeria out that they are able to do things like that? Far from it! It is because they decided to build a city that the world will envy for themselves. They decided to build a wonder for the whole world and they set out to do so.

We must arise and build Nigeria as well. We must build our roads. We must re-orientate our people on the use of the roads. Don't tell me that it is the government that has failed to give us good roads because that is far from the truth. While the government has its blame, the fact remains that the Nigerian populace haven't been educated and trained on how to use and preserve her roads. Or was it the government that loosened and took away the bolts of the Niger Bridge several years ago? Is it the government that comes out at mid night to destroy major roads leading from city to city so they could come out during the day to trade and sell stuffs in traffic jams caused by them?

Maybe you are the one to take it upon yourself to re-educate the Nigerian populace on why they shouldn't destroy and vandalize our roads.

HOW TO IDENTIFY YOUR MOUNTAIN

Evidently, the list of mountains of problems facing our country that I have talked about isn't exactly exhaustive. They are just to give you an idea of the challenges before us and how that we have to begin doing something about them now rather than just sitting and saying "only God can save Nigeria".

While I believe that many people would have already seen an area where they would like to get involved in to change our country, some others may still have doubts and uncertainties. So I want to show you how to identify your area of assignment and sphere of operations. I want to give you a kind of guideline to decide on what you should do to contribute your own quota to the development and improvement of our dear country.

The Areas That Annoy You

You see, you have been perfectly created in a way that the purpose for your creation is always groaning for expression within you. That is why one of the ways to discover an area of life you are called to is to find out what annoys you.

You will find that you have an unusual anger about the problems you are called to solve. You will have a kind of anger that is hard to explain and resolve. The only way that anger can ever be resolved is for you to do something in the area of that anger. It is only when you set out to start doing something about that thing that angers you that you begin to find peace.

My question to you right now is: what annoys you about the Nigerian state today? Which sector or area of the country gets to you the most? Is it the political mess we have found ourselves in or the dilapidated state of things in our hospitals? It could be the lackadaisical attitude to work or the traffic problem that annoys you the most. Whichever area it is that you get angry the most, that is an indication of an area for which God has placed the solution in you. Get to work already following the step by step plan I outline for you in this book.

The Problems You Have gone through and Solved

Many of us have not only suffered stuffs in our lives but we have gone through a lot. We suffered and suffered until we found a way out of the suffering. We have gone through the tunnel already and looking back in retrospect, there is so much we can say to people who are right there where we used to be.

Have you been a prostitute before and now a responsible citizen of the society? Have you been a drug addict and are now clean? Were you a school dropout who now have a second degree or even a PhD? What is it you have gone through and came out successful at? Can't you begin offering your experience to help others in the same position you used to be? Who is better positioned to help solve that problem than someone like you who has been there before?

Sometimes, God allows us to go through certain difficulties and unpleasant situations so that we can be better equipped to bring about salvation in that area for other people. He lets us pass through so we can become a guide that will show others the way.

I want you to take a careful and critical look at your life all these years and identify that problem you surmounted successfully that is still a problem in our country then note down the exact steps it took you to pass through. Then develop a plan to share the same secrets with others to help them do the same. Build a platform or NGO for the same purpose and get to work saving millions of Nigerians from the same issues you once suffered from.

You can't have that wealth of experience and say you don't know what God has called you to do. You can't have all that knowledge and still be in doubt as to what your calling might be. Please swing into action with immediate effect my dear.

The Areas You Are Passionate About

Passion! Passion! Passion! We all have it. Every single one of us has one thing or the other that we are passionate about. There is something that we love and enjoy doing so much that it feels like second nature to us. I mean something you get involved with and everything else just fades away.

Passion is one of those pointers that God puts in us to lead us towards what He wants us to do with our lives. So find yours. Discover what you are passionate about doing. Something that when you get involved with it, you are literally lost in a world of your own.

Then consider how that passion measures up with the problems we have in Nigeria. How can that passion be converted into a solution? How can that passion be used to bring about some kind of change or transformation? What can you do with that passion that will result in the common good of us all as a nation? That might just be what God has placed you here to accomplish for Him. That might just be your own mountain and area of operation.

Don't say you don't know what to do to bring about salvation to Nigeria when you are passionate about something that is a problem in Nigeria. Don't say you can't do much when you are already in love with something that can make a difference in our country.

If you are a stickler for orderliness, use that passion to bring about some order in a sphere of life that you choose. If you are a chronic keeper of time, why not use that to teach workers or students how to value and keep to time? Do you have an idea what a difference that will make on our country in the long run? If you are a lover of photography, what about teaching others how to take cool pictures and creating jobs for them that way? If you are a computer guru or you are passionate about technology, why don't you use that to improve the computer literacy in the country?

Whatever your passion is, the possibilities are just endless. There are a myriad of things you can possibly do to make an impact with your God-given passion my dear.

You should begin to think how all that can be transformed into something that will in turn improve the country. You can use your passion to create jobs for others. You can use your passion to create products and services that others will love and appreciate. The ball is completely in your court but make sure you do something with that passion and improve lives around the country.

WHAT TO DO AFTER DISCOVERING YOUR MOUNTAIN AND CALLING

Alright, now you have discovered your mountain. You have found out where you are supposed to function and represent God in thus, bringing about change and development to Nigeria. So what next? What should you do now that you know where you are supposed to serve? That is what I want to tell you about now. I have a list of 5 things you should do when you get to your promised land.

1. Research The Top Problems There

The major reason why many people find it difficult to perform in their places of assignment is because they don't know where to start from. This has been the case with many of my mentees over the years. They feel overwhelmed about the problems of the society that they wonder where to begin from. This shouldn't be the case at all.

What you have to do is to begin by researching the problems of that sphere. Do not assume that you already know them. Do your due diligence. Ask the right questions of the right people and make sure you come up with real problems. You can start by finding answers to the following questions:

- What keeps people in that sphere awake at night?
- What are the pains they go through?
- What gets them angry?
- What are their frustrations?
- What are they unhappy about?
- What are their dreams and aspirations?
- What do they need the most?

These will help you come up with a broad idea of what the problems there are. And like they say, a problem known is half solved already!

2. Come Up With a Plan Or Strategy

Now that you know the problems in the sphere of life that you have been called into, the next thing you have to do is to come up with a plan for tackling them. You want to draw up your plan of action on how you intend to bring solution to these problems.

Your plan doesn't have to be so elaborate that it scares you to death instead of inspiring action in you. The plan just has got to be concise and detailed enough to gain the attention of your sphere. You want to make sure it's a plan that can inspire hope in anyone who sees it.

So in crafting out this plan, you want to ask yourself the following questions:

- What is the future I am promising or bringing into this sphere?
- What will it take to move from the present state of things to the future that I envisage?
- How long do I think it will take me to start seeing visible and measurable results?
- What will I have to do every day to get these results?

3. Come Up With Examples And Models

Just before you swing into full action effecting changes in your sphere, you might want to take your research a step further. Chances are that there are other people, corporate bodies and countries that have tackled the same problem sometime in the past. There is every likelihood that the result you are trying to achieve in your sphere of influence right now has already been achieved somewhere else. So what you want to do now is to find out how they achieved that result in other places. You also want to find out how they managed to sustain the result in places where they have had that for several years.

Remember that you don't just want to start a movement for the fun of it or the sake of just doing something. We are talking about taking calculated steps for a specific purpose. You don't just want to build, you want to build to last. So you should find out how it was built in other places and how it is being maintained in the long run.

4. Become The Best

This is something that is so important and I want you to get it. The world we live in right now has no space for "mediocres". There is no space for second fiddles and people who just want to barely make it. It is time we inculcated excellence into our culture and tradition as a country. We must become excellence minded and determine to deliver only excellent results.

As such, as part of our research of what worked in other places, we should also find out what the best is right now. We should know what the record on ground is and our target should be to beat the best record. For crying out loud, there is no reason why we should be involved with something and be okay to do it less than the English people or the Americans will do it. We shouldn't be deceived by the fact that we are the giant of Africa because the world is way bigger than Africa. It's a global world we are competing against my dear.

I like the story I heard about the ruler of Dubai – Sheikh Mohammed Bin Rashid. When they were planning to build the Burj Khalifa, the engineer in charge brought a plan for a 90 floor building to him. But Sheikh Mohammed rejected the plan. He told him to go and make something better! Later the engineer came back with another plan and Sheikh Mohammed asked him how much taller than the current tallest building is that? He only approved the plan after the engineer came up with something that was 40% taller than the tallest building! Currently, that building is 198m and 35 floors taller than the second tallest building in the world! That's what being the best is all about my dear.

I challenge you to get every training necessary and come up with something that can only be compared to the best in the world. Whatever field or sphere of life you are involved with, only think in terms of the best in the world.

It is high time "Aba Made" stopped meaning inferior quality. We can change that. We can make our very own Aba a production center that manufactures goods worthy of export.

That alone can go a long way to improve the economy, the value of our currency and so much more.

5. Develop Your Own 10 Commandments/Policies

Why is it that sometimes, we find that when an individual is in office, things work well but the moment they are out, things kind of revert back to the way they used to be before? It is because even though the person was effective in changing things, he did not build systems. He did not build structures to uphold what he already started.

This is the reason countries have constitutions and companies have policies. These ensure that no matter who is involved, things will always work in a certain way that has been predetermined by the country or organization.

So now that you can see what others did to get to where they are right now and you are all set to begin taking steps towards implementing the same in your sphere, be sure to also set up policies and commandments that will ensure things remain the same. Your goal is not just to change the way things are right now but to affect the way things are done entirely.

For example, someone can come up with a brilliant idea to clean up our streets. That would be nice and welcome but if there is no system or structure in place to ensure that what made the streets dirty in the first place is not repeated, that idea will only be short lived.

That is why I say that the real change will only come when we have set up structures to prevent their re-occurrence. This is another reason you have to ensure that you do your research and home work well. If you know the cause of a thing, it is by far easier to prevent its re-occurrence that way.

Conclusion and
Final Thoughts

Conclusion and Final Thoughts

Only God can save Nigeria? Hmm, maybe... Maybe God can actually save Nigeria, but, friends, that will not be before we have done our absolute best to fix Nigeria. We must put everything that He has already given us to good use before we can turn around to say that "only God can save Nigeria".

In fact, I can guarantee that the only reason people ever say that only God can save Nigeria is because they don't want to take responsibility for anything. If you dare got up and started doing something from your end to save Nigeria, you will definitely come to the conclusion that God has already brought salvation to Nigeria and you are definitely one of the channels for that salvation.

God indeed could show up, but we must first show good stewardship. God can manifest his salvation plan but it has to begin by us taking good care of our land. We must prove to God that we have done all that depends on us. Then what we cannot do He would come and do for us.

> "And we owe science to the combined energies of individual men of genius, rather than to any tendency to progress inherent in civilization". (CHAUNCEY WRIGHT)

Chauncey Wright is trying to tell us that nothing progresses by itself, in this he concurs with the great English scientist Sir Isaac Newton that says there is no effect without a cause, if there is progress anywhere it is because there have been people who worked for it, and not just prayed for it. Everywhere there has been development in the world, it was because men took action. They did something more than praying to bring about the change they required.

So it is time we did the same. It is time we went beyond just praying and hoping that our prayers will change things. When we have prayed, we must then get up and do something. We must get up and take steps to bring our prayers to pass. In fact, the real proof that you prayed and believed that your prayer was effective is what you do after the prayer.

So far, I hope you have enjoyed reading this book as well as I have enjoyed writing it. I hope you have begun to see the enormous potentials and possibilities for our dear nation if we all put our hands on the plough. However, at this point in our discussion, I think it is appropriate that I bring in something I call a word of caution. A word of caution because I know that many religious people will like to quote a scripture in the book of Daniel to discredit all that we have been talking about.

"This decision is by the decree of the watchers, And the sentence by the word of the holy ones, In order that the living may know That the Most High rules in the kingdom of men, gives it to whomever He will, And sets over it the lowest of men". (DAN 4:17)

People have read this to mean that there is no need for us to do anything because God has everything under his control. They have interpreted it to mean that even in the kingdom of men, God rules and reigns. So we better all sit back and allow Him do what he decides is right for us all.

However, something I will like for you to note here is the fact that when the scripture says that God rules in the kingdom of men, it was as a lesson to Nebuchadnezzar who tried to remove God all together from his affairs. He became proud and full of himself that he began to feel like he could get God out of the city completely. That was when God decided to teach him a lesson.

We endeavour not to fall into this trap either just like many nations in the world today. They are saying they don't need God and everything depends on them only. But that is so wrong. No, no, no, no!!! While God has entrusted us with taking care of things here, we must always acknowledge that He is the source of all wisdom and strength with which we perform and function.

In such cases where men try to keep God out of the affairs of the land, He would show up sooner or later to make them know that no one can bypass Him. That is when He shows up and sets whomever He wills to take over the reins.

In other words, when people who should have taken the responsibility to make things happen in a country fail, when people God has placed to bring about growth and development fail to do so, God can always find Himself a replacement. He can always get another person to get into that same shoe they are in and deliver the desired results.

Whatever it is you have identified that you are called to and passionate about doing, I want these words to ring loud in your mind. I want you to remember that God is counting on you. And I want you to know that if you decide to ignore Him and go about your own business, He will always find a way out. He will always find someone else to get the job done in time.

Therefore, don't wait any longer. Get moving right now into the sphere of life that you are fitted to make a difference and let us begin to record victories upon victories on your account. Let the nation begin to experience that growth and development that you have been fitted to bring about. Let the Nigerian people smile again because you are alive.

We should however not seek to abdicate our duties to God, asking God to come and do what we are supposed to do. We can't ask God to come and fix our nation while we have not done our absolute best. Give it your very best and leave the rest for God to bless and multiply!

MAY GOD NOT REGRET THAT HE MADE YOU A NIGERIAN!

One of the most pathetic reports I have heard was the report God made of a man named Saul in the bible. Saul had been made king over Israel to carry out God's instructions in the land but he failed woefully! Instead of living for what God set him there for, Saul had his own agenda. He lived for every other reason save the real reason why he was made king.

In talking about him and what he had done, God's response was this:

> *"I regret that I made Saul king, for he has turned away from following Me and has not carried out My instructions." So Samuel became angry and cried out to the LORD all night. "* (1 SAM 15:11)

Dear friend, please do not make the same mistake Saul made in your life. Do not forfeit the real assignment and purpose of your life for religion and the deception of men. Do not allow yourself to fall victim to the schemes of men who have lost God's purpose and direction.

It is time you stood up and fulfilled your mission on earth. Particularly, it is time you began to fulfil your mission as a Nigerian. Go out there, find that problem you were designed and fitted to fix, set up your platform or organization to do that and swing straight into action my dear.

May God never feel sorry that He made you a Nigerian and gave you an assignment to fulfil in Nigeria in Jesus name.

Thank you for reading this far. I really can't wait to hear what becomes of you through the application of these laws and secrets. Feel free to write me at any time to my personal email: pastor@godembassy.org

You can also avail yourself of other training materials of mine available on my blog at www.SundayAdelajaBlog.com

Sunday Adelaja,
For The Love of God, Church and Nation

About Pastor
Sunday Adelaja

Sunday Adelaja is the founder and senior pastor of the Embassy of God in Kiev Ukraine and the author of more than 300 books which are translated in several languages including Chinese, German, French, Arabic, etc.

A fatherless child from a 40 hut village in Nigeria, Sunday was recruited by communist Russia to ignite a revolution, instead he was saved just before leaving for the USSR where he secretly trained himself in the Bible while earning a Master's degree in journalism. By age thirty-three he had built the largest church in Europe.

Today, his church in Kiev has planted over a thousand daughter churches in over fifty countries of the world. Right now they plant four new churches every week. He is known to be the only person in the world pastoring a cross cultural church where 99% of his twenty five thousand members are white Caucasians.

His work has been widely reported by world media outlets like Washington Post, The wall street Journal, Forbes, New York times, Associated Press, Reuters, CNN, BBC, German, Dutch, French National television, etc.

Pastor Sunday had the opportunity to speak on a number of occasions in the United Nations. In 2007 he had the rare privilege of opening the United States Senate with prayers. He has spoken in the Israeli Knesset and the Japanese parliament along with several other countries. Pastor Sunday is known as an expert in national transformation through biblical principles and values.

Pastor Sunday is happily married to his "princess' Pastor Bose Adelaja. They are blessed with three children, Perez, Zoe and Pearl.

Follow Sunday Adelaja
On Social Media

Subscribe And Read Pastor Sunday's Blog:
www.sundayadelajablog.com

Follow These Links And Listen To Over 200 Of Pastor Sunday's Messages Free Of Charge:
http://sundayadelajablog.com/content/

Follow Pastor Sunday on Twitter:
www.twitter.com/official_pastor

Join Pastor Sunday's Facebook page to stay in touch:
www.facebook.com/pastor.sunday.adelaja

Visit our websites for more information about Pastor Sunday's ministry:
http://www.godembassy.com
http://www.pastorsunday.com
http://sundayadelaja.de

BEST SELLING BOOKS BY DR. SUNDAY ADELAJA

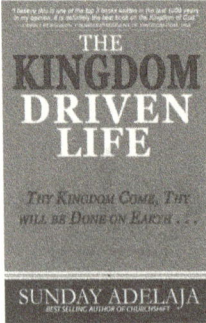

The Kingdom Driven Life:
Thy Kingdom Come, Thy Will be Done on
Earth
(Best seller)

Myles Munroe:
... Finding Answers To Why Good People
Die Tragic And Early Deaths

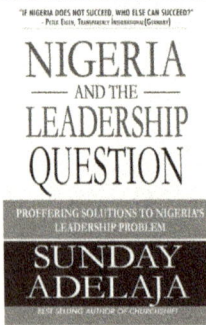

Nigeria And
The Leadership Question:
Proffering Solutions To Nigeria's Leadership
Problem

Olorunwa (There Is Sunday):
Portrait Of Sunday Adelaja.
The Roads Of Life.

AVAILABLE ON AMAZON AND OKADABOOKS.COM

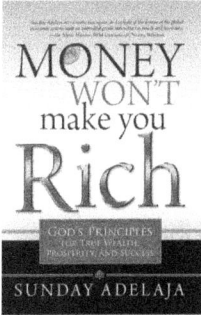

Money Won't Make You Rich:
God's Principles for True Wealth, Prosperity, and Success

Who Am I? Why Am I here?:
How to discover your purpose and calling in life

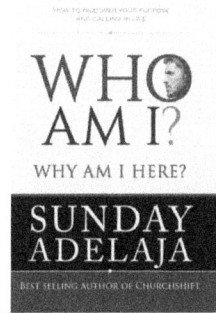

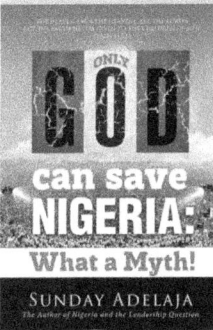

Only God Can Save Nigeria:
What a Myth?

Church Shift:
Revolutionizing Your Faith, Church, and Life for the 21st Century

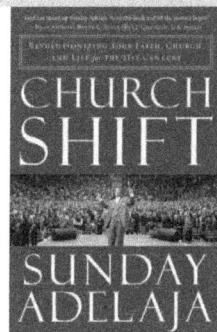

... and many more.

Contact

For distribution or to order bulk copies of this book,
please contact us:

USA
CORNERSTONE PUBLISHING
info@thecornerstonepublishers.com
+1 (516) 547-4999
www.thecornerstonepublishers.com

AFRICA
Sunday Adelaja Media Ltd.
Email: btawolana@hotmail.com
+2348187518530, +2348097721451, +2348034093699.

LONDON, UK
Abraham Great
abrahamagreat@gmail.com
+44 7590 110001, +44-1908538141

KIEV, UKRAINE
pa@godembassy.org
Mobile: +380674401958

www.ingramcontent.com/pod-product-compliance
Lightning Source LLC
Chambersburg PA
CBHW031250090426
42742CB00007B/398